Living Jewishly
A Snapshot of a Generation

JEWISH IDENTITIES IN POST MODERN SOCIETY

ACADEMIC
STUDIES
PRESS

LIVING JEWISHLY

A Snapshot of a Generation

An anthology edited by *Stefanie Pervos Bregman*

Boston
2012

Library of Congress Cataloging-in-Publication Data:
A catalog record for this book is available from the Library of Congress.

ISBN 978-1-618111-63-0 (hardback)
ISBN 978-1-618112-64-4 (paperback)
Book design by Alyssa Zeller

Jewish United Fund/Jewish Federation
of Metropolitan Chicago

Published by Academic Studies Press in 2012
28 Montfern Avenue
Brighton, MA 02135, USA
press@academicstudiespress.com
www. academicstudiespress.com

CONTENTS

CONTENTS

Stories come to us in so many ways. They are the tales grandparents tell us; they are the words of "black fire" leaping from ancient scrolls. The best stories we harvest from our own experience, a new vintage that over time will become the sacred wine staining our family *Haggadot*. What is a Jewish story? In this deft collection Stefanie Pervos Bregman gathers together storytellers who relate their journeys, and in the telling map for us what, for a young generation of Jews, is the landscape of Jewish identity. Here we learn what matters, what resonates, what sticks. The Jewish United Fund/ Jewish Federation of Metropolitan Chicago is proud to have supported Ms. Bregman in this effort, for she not only is a fine storyteller herself but also is a master enabler of other storytellers. The stories that endure and the love in their telling will make the Jewish future as fertile as our past. May this book be a seed.

    —Aaron B. Cohen, Vice President of Communications for the Jewish United Fund/ Jewish Federation of Metropolitan Chicago

I AM JEWISH

By Andrew Lustig

I AM THE COLLECTIVE PRIDE AND EXCITEMENT THAT is felt when we find out that that new actor, that great athlete, his chief of staff...is Jewish.

And I am the collective guilt and shame that is felt when we find out that that serial killer, that Ponzi schemer, that wife beater...is Jewish.

I am the Jewish star tattooed on the chest of the teenager who chooses to rebel against his parents' and grandparents' warnings of a lonely goyim cemetery by embracing that same Judaism and making permanent his Jewish identity.

I am all the words in Yiddish I've been called all my life that I still don't understand.

I am going to all three Phish shows this weekend.

I am my melody of Adon Olam. I am *my* melody of Adon Olam. The words may be the same but I am *my* melody of Adon Olam.

I am not getting bar mitzvahed. I am a Bar Mitzvah.

I am a concept foreign to the rest of the world. I am not Judaism. I am sleep-away camp.

I am your grandmother who's seen Chortkov and Auschwitz, who's seen '49, '67, and '73 and who's tired of trying to make peace with those people who just want to blow up buses and destroy her people.

I am the 19-year-old who's seen *Budrus*, *Don't Mess With the Zohan*, and *Waltz with Bashir* and who thinks— who *knows*—peace is possible.

I am the complicated reason you take the cheese off of the burger you eat at the Saturday morning tailgate.

I am constantly struggling to understand my Jewish identity outside of religion.

I am the Torah and not the Old Testament.

I am a Kippah and not a Skull Cap.

I am a Jew and not an Israeli.

5,000 years old...not 60.

A religion, not a country.

I am never asked if I have horns or a pot of gold, if I rule the world or why I killed Jesus. I am asked where my black hat is, if I really get eight presents on my Christmas, why my sideburns aren't super long, and if I've really never tried bacon.

I am asked what a gefilte fish is. I say, "I don't know. I don't like it. Nobody does. But we eat it because it's what we do."

I am asked if my dad's a lawyer. I say, "No...my mom is...my dad's an accountant."

I am asked if my grandparents were in the Holocaust as if it were a movie. "Yeah, they were. But luckily they were also on Schindler's List."

I am on JDate and not Match.com because, well, it's just easier that way.

I am that feeling of obligation to buy the Dead Sea salt at the mall kiosk because you know the woman's Israeli.

I am an IDF sweatshirt and the chai around your neck. I am a $100 challah cover you will never use and a five shekel piece of red string you will wear until it withers away. I am your Hebrew name. I am your Israeli cousins. I am your Torah portion and your 13 candles. I am your bat mitzvah dress and the cute Israeli soldier on your Birthright trip.

I am 18 when I discover that Israel is not actually a garden of Eden of milk and honey where Jews of all backgrounds, ethnicities, and styles of worship come together—eternally happy and appreciative—to do a constant Hora in the streets of the promised land.

I am still confident that it will be.

I am the way your stomach forgets to be hungry and your lungs forget to breathe when the Rabbi commands the final Tekiah Gadolah and an entire congregation—a congregation that is not any one synagogue but an entire people—listens to what on January 1st is a ball dropping in Times Square, but today—any day in late September or early October for the 5770th time—is a Ram's horn being blown into for what seems like 10 minutes, like the eight days the oil burned, and how David defeated Goliath, and how Moses parted the seas...it would have been enough, Dayenu. How we won the war, and how your grandparents survived—Nes Gadol Haya Sham—Shana Tova—time for bagels and lox because I am Jewish.

PROLOGUE

IN THE JEWISH COMMUNAL WORLD, ENGAGING 20- and 30-somethings is a hot button issue: How do we get young Jews to feel connected to Israel? To affiliate with traditional Jewish institutions? To care about Jewish continuity, ritual and tradition?

As a member of this elusive generation myself, I live and breathe these questions in my personal life, in my work as a Jewish professional at the Jewish United Fund/ Jewish Federation of Metropolitan Chicago, as the editor of Oy!Chicago[1], and as a graduate of the Spertus Institute's Master of Arts in Jewish Professional Studies program.

I hoped to get some answers by going straight to the source, and sought out to compile a collection of personal essays and memoirs from Jewish 20- and 30-somethings across the country. In mid-August of 2010, I sent out a call for stories to my contacts at Jewish publications and asked friends to forward the request and post it on Facebook and Twitter: *"Are you a Jewish 20- or 30-something with a story to tell? Do you want to be part of a collection of voices that together tell the unique story of our generation?"*[2] I hoped someone, anyone, would respond.

They did.

By my deadline about six weeks later, I had received close to 50 submissions—all remarkable, rich, wonderful and more diverse than I could have ever imagined. I found

---

[1] Oy!Chicago (www.oychicago.com) is a blog geared toward engaging Jewish 20- and 30-somethings in Chicago.

[2] See Appendix A.

that from these essays, I could identify nine common threads among the Jewish 20- and 30-somethings who responded. But before I delve into the lessons to be garnered from these stories, first, I will look at this demographic through the lens of researchers, journalists and sociologists. Afterward, I will explore what we can learn about Jewish 20- and 30-somethings through their personal stories.

ZOOMING IN ON THE RESEARCH

So what does the picture of an American Jewish 20- or 30-something look like today? Over the past decade, figuring out what makes members of this generation tick has become a genre in and of itself.

A New Focus: Redefining "Jewish"

Today, Jews in their 20s and 30s *choose* Judaism because of "what it has to offer intellectually, spiritually and emotionally."[3] They want meaningful Jewish experiences where they can find engaging and fulfilling communities and networks, and if existing institutions—i.e. synagogues, Federations, JCCs—can't keep up, young Jews will simply create their own programs.

A 2007 study by Steven M. Cohen and Ari Y. Kelman, "The Continuity of Discontinuity," found that "Jewish communities are in the process of inventing and reinventing themselves in order to continue contributing to the conversations of their members."[4] As a result, many new Jewish programs and initiatives have been launched with an eye toward satisfying the next generation, since many of the programs are driven by Jewish 20- and 30-somethings.[5]

This generation of Jews is different from their parents and grandparents in many ways—and yet just like their parents and grandparents did, young Jews today are redefining what it means to be Jewish. This age group has never known a world without the State of Israel, is generations

---

[3] Ethan Tucker. "What Independent Minyanim Teach Us About the Next Generation of Jewish Communities," *Zeek* (Spring 2007): www.zeek.net/801tucker/.

[4] Steven M. Cohen and Ari Y. Kelman, "The Continuity of Discontinuity" (New York: Andrea and Charles Bronfman Philanthropies, 2007): 7.

[5] Jack Wertheimer, "Generations of Change: How Leaders in their Twenties and Thirties are Reshaping American Jewish Life" (The AVI CHAI FOUNDATION, Sept 2010): 1.

removed from the Holocaust and, while exposed to some anti-Semitism, most have never personally experienced any anti-Semitic sentiment. For the most part, being Jewish does not impact their day-to-day lives and activities, unless, of course, they want it to.

> For the younger Jews of today who are fully in the mainstream of American life, there is no longer a feeling of forced choice between being Jewish and becoming American. Being American has simply become the default position, and any active relationship to Jewishness requires either prior commitment (i.e. a history of involvement or prior socialization) or an act of will.[6]

In a 2004 *Washington Post* article, Alicia Svigals, a pioneer of the Jewish music scene, put it this way: "We're not vulnerable immigrants anymore," she says in the article. "And so you can say 'shalom'—because you don't have to worry. What's being defied is no longer anti-Semitism and the hostile, non-Jewish world."[7]

The Sovereign Self

In the 2000 book, *The Jew Within*, Steven M. Cohen and Arnold M. Eisen outline an argument that "today's Jews, like their peers in other religious traditions, have turned inward in the search for meaning."[8] Meaningful Jewish experiences, they argue, occur within the private sphere. "American Jews, we believe, enact and express their decisions about Judaism predominantly in the intimate spaces of love and family, friendship and reflection" and "the principal [Jewish] authority is the sovereign self."[9]

After conducting interviews with Jewish men and women aged 30 to 50—just a bit older than today's 20- and 30-somethings, Cohen and Eisen determined that even the most committed Jews "decide week by week, year by year, which rituals they will observe and how they will observe them. They also repeatedly reconsider which organizations and charities they will join or support, and to what degree; which beliefs they will

---

[6] Bethamie Horowitz, *Connections and Journeys: Assessing Critical Opportunities for Enhancing Jewish Identity* (New York: UJA-Federation, 2000), v.

[7] Carol Eisenberg, "Young, Jewish and…Cool: Music, Multiculturalism Help Generation Reconnect with Ethnic Identity," WashingtonPost.com 17 April 2004, 5, Aug. 2010.

[8] Steven M. Cohen and Arnold M. Eisen, *The Jew Within: Self, Family and Community in America* (Bloomington and Indianapolis: Indiana University Press, 2000): 2.

[9] Cohen, Eisen, *The Jew Within*, 1.

hold, which loyalties they will acknowledge. The self is and must remain autonomous and sovereign."[10] In "A Congregation of One," a 2002 study by Jeffrey Arnett and Lene Arnett Jensen, the findings were similar: "Religious traditions have become 'symbolic toolboxes' from which individuals can draw without accepting as a whole the worldview that was historically part of the religion."[11]

All Eyes on "Me"

Today's young people—from child-aged through 40—have been labeled "Generation Me," a stereotype that implies they place themselves as individuals before anything, or anyone, else. Jews in their 20s and 30s are no exception. Immune to the rigidity of traditional Jewish life, they pick and choose what, when and how to live Jewishly. For some in their 20s and 30s, this means joining the conversation online through blogs and social networks, for others joining an independent minyan, and for others it's cultural—going to Jewish-themed or sponsored parties or concerts, joining JDate, or simply eating Chinese food on Christmas.

However Jewish 20- and 30-somethings choose to express their Jewishness, they do so in a way that works for them personally. In "The Continuity of Discontinuity," Cohen and Kelman profiled four initiatives spearheaded by young Jews—Ikar, a spiritual community based in LA; Storahtelling, a nonprofit musical and dramatic company that promotes Jewish cultural literacy through theatrical performances; JDub records; and The Salon, a Toronto-based place for open and honest Jewish discussion. In the study, Cohen and Kelman report that those involved in these new initiatives seek to "make Judaism mine."[12] Because existing institutions and programming did not meet their needs, the founders of these initiatives sought to "create space for conversation to happen."[13]

These days, we can no longer measure Jewish identity based on how often one goes to synagogue, or how large their donation to Jewish federations or philanthropies. So researchers today are looking to what is personally meaningful to each individual, emphasizing "diverse ways

---

[10] Cohen, Eisen, *The Jew Within*, 7.

[11] Jeffrey Jensen Arnett and Lene Arnett Jensen, "A Congregation of One: Individualized Religious Beliefs Among Emerging Adults," *Journal of Adolescent Research*, Vol 17 No 5 (September 2002): 453.

[12] Cohen and Kelman, "The Continuity of Discontinuity," 21.

[13] Cohen and Kelman, "The Continuity of Discontinuity," 33.

of being Jewish, rather than on better or worse levels of Jewishness."[14] For example, Beth Cousens wrote her doctoral dissertation—a case study of a synagogue-based community for 20-and 30-somethings—to better understand "the process through which adults in their 20s and 30s discover their senses of their Jewish selves, and the experiences that transform their understanding of their own Jewishness."[15]

Emerging Adulthood

Perhaps some of this attitude can be explained by what Jeffrey Arnett calls "emerging adulthood," a new phenomenon and life stage between adolescence and adulthood which generally lasts from the late teens through the late 20s and sometimes longer. Many of today's Jewish 20-and 30-somethings are experiencing this new life stage. Emerging adulthood, Arnett says, is a period characterized by the following: 1) identity exploration—emerging adults spend this time figuring out who they are 2) instability—many emerging adults move from job to job, and city to city; 3) Because it typically comes before marriage and children, it is considered the most self-focused age of life 4) the age of transition—when one is neither child or adult and finally 5) the age of possibilities.[16] "There has been a profound change in how young people view the meaning and value of becoming an adult and entering the adult roles of spouse and parent," Arnett says.[17] Many young people feel that getting married in their early 20s would cut short their opportunity to experience "independence and spontaneity—the very qualities that are so attractive about the emerging adult years."[18] They also want to get their own lives in order before committing themselves to someone else. For many though, age 30 is the deadline for marriage, because it "fits with the rest of their plan."[19]

> As a kid, I grew up thinking my life would turn out a certain way. At 34, I thought I would be married with three kids, just like my mom and dad. I thought I would have a Jewish husband and we would have couple

[14] Horowitz, *Connections and Journeys,* 183.
[15] Beth Cousens, *Shifting Social Networks: Studying the Jewish Growth of Adults in Their Twenties and Thirties* (PhD Dissertation, Brandeis University, 2008): 6.
[16] Jeffrey Jensen Arnett, *Emerging Adulthood: The Winding Road from the Late Teens through the Twenties* (New York: Oxford University Press, 2004): 8.
[17] Arnett, *Emerging Adulthood,* 6.
[18] Arnett, *Emerging Adulthood,* 101.
[19] Arnett, *Emerging Adulthood,* 103.

friends and I'd pick up their kids at soccer practice and they would pick up mine . . . And so the day he proposed I viewed it as part of the plan, even though I knew the relationship wouldn't work out . . . I was 26 years old. Kid 1 at 29, Kid 2 at 31 and Kid 3 at 33. Perfect.[20]

Searching for Community

Cohen and Eisen argue that if the "first language" of today's Jews is individuals, their "second language" is community.[21] In fact, "Generation Me" has also been called "Generation We." Throughout their journeys to discover their own Jewish identities, Jewish 20- and 30-somethings are also searching for meaning, community and a sense of belonging.

In *Big Questions, Worthy Dreams: Mentoring Young Adults in Their Search for Meaning, Purpose, and Faith*, author Sharon D. Parks talks of the power of the tribe as balancing two great yearnings: the yearning for one's own power to make a difference and the yearning for belonging, connection, inclusion, relationship and intimacy.

> The young adult most thrives when there is access to a network of belonging centered in the strength of worthy meanings that impart a sense of distance from the conventions of the young adult's past and from the larger society with which the young adult must still negotiate terms of entry.[22]

In her search for belonging, Caren Friedman found Jewish community in an unlikely setting:

> About two years ago, I was fortunate enough to be invited to join a group of girls for dinner at a friend's apartment. In her living room, amongst veggies and six varieties of hummus, sat what appeared to be a random assortment of women . . . The common thread among us: seeking connection . . . We have created our own community . . . I realize that "Girls' Night" is not an official congregation or dues-collecting organization. And I am confident that I will eventually find those types of outlets again. But in the meantime, as I continue my cultural and spiritual exploration, this little pocket of Jewish women is very welcome indeed.[23]

---

[20] Sharna Marcus, "The Plan," p. 7.
[21] Cohen, Eisen, *The Jew Within*, 7.
[22] Sharon Daloz Parks, *Big Questions, Worthy Dreams: Mentoring Young Adults in Their Search for Meaning, Purpose, and Faith*, (San Francisco: Josey-Bass, 2000): 96.
[23] Caren Friedman, "34 is the New 'Tween,'" p. 46.

Because 20- and 30-somethings often do not like the impersonal feel of large institutional events, or events that feel like "meat markets," some young Jews, like Caren, look to smaller groups to find their community. "Disaffected from large social institutions, the Birthright Israel generation[24] looks to smaller social settings and informal networks of friends for a sense of community. Watters[25] (2003) coined the phrase 'urban tribes' to describe the family-like role played by small groups of peers in supporting individuals through emerging adulthood."[26]

So what does all this mean for Jewish life in America? For one, it means that what were once central vehicles for Jewish life and identity—Jewish institutions—must make room and make way for new focal points.

In the Background: The Role of Jewish Institutions

According to Arnett, the individualism valued by many emerging adults makes them skeptical of religious institutions and wary of being part of one.[27] As a result, many are disinterested in traditional Jewish institutional life—federations, synagogues, etc. The 2000/01 National Jewish population study reported that of unmarried Jews ages 25 to 29 in the U.S., 22% belong to synagogues, 5% pay dues to JCCs, 7% are members of other Jewish organizations and only 5% contribute $100 or more to their local federation campaign.[28]

So why the disconnect from institutional life? Some young Jews may not like the feeling of being told where to give their money and when, or when to pray and where. For some, "that which they experienced as children has resulted for them in mistrust of traditional religious leaders and interaction with religious institutions that is unique to their generation."[29] A 2006 Reboot study by Anna Greenberg, "Grande Soy Vanilla Latte With Cinnamon, No Foam...Jewish Identity and Community in a Time of Un-limited Choices" gives three very different explanations of a disconnect from

---

[24] This refers to the more than 150,000 young adults from North America who are alumni of the Taglit-Birthright Israel program, see Fern Chertok, Theodore Sasson, Leonard Saxe, "Tourists, Travelers, and Citizens: Jewish Engagement of Young Adults in Four Centers of North American Jewish Life" (Cohen Center for Modern Jewish Studies, March 2009).

[25] This refers to Ethan Watters, *Urban tribes: A generation redefines friendship, family, and commitment* (Bloomsbury, London 2003).

[26] Chertok, Sasson, and Saxe, "Tourists, Travelers, and Citizens,"18.

[27] Arnett, *Emerging Adulthood*, 173.

[28] Cohen and Kelman, "The Continuity of Discontinuity," 16.

[29] Cousens, *Shifting Social Networks*, 69.

institutional life that is more pronounced. First, young Jews today—like many of their predecessors—often "voice cynical attitudes" about agendas they see as catering to the elite. Second, some think they will be judged for "not being Jewish enough"[30] in their knowledge of Jewish ritual. Finally, as young people become interested in more general social justice causes—like the environment or human rights—they may be hesitant to get involved in an organization that serves only Jewish interests.[31] They balk at umbrella organizations and want to direct their money and support to specific causes.

In "Grande Soy" Greenberg mentions casual ways young Jews practice Judaism, even something as simple as having their friends over for Friday night dinner.[32] "These informal articulations of 'being Jewish' often involve specific, organized, broadly sectarian events or gatherings, but not formal ceremonies at synagogues."[33]

But, the study points out, despite their weak institutional ties, these Jews have strong cultural Jewish identities:

> What stops young Jews from greater participation in Jewish institutions runs the gamut...But to be clear, their lack of involvement is not because of a weak Jewish identity. Young Jews do not lack self-confidence about their Jewishness, nor do they lack connection to their families or the values with which they grew up, nor do they feel disconnected from Jewish peoplehood. Rather, in their views, the institutionalized Jewish community does not meet their needs or speak to their interests as young people.[34]

Also important to note is that despite their apparent disdain for institutions, funding for most "non-establishment" programming comes from established organizations, such as federations or foundations, as Jack Wertheimer reports in a new study on the next generation of Jewish leaders released in 2010: "For all the talk of a clear division between programs for young Jews and the established community, leaders of start-ups privately admit they could not function without support from established organizations and foundations." Wertheimer argues that the process is really intergenerational:

---

[30] Anna Greenberg, "Grande Soy Vanilla Latte with Cinnamon, No Foam: Jewish Identity and Community in a Time of Unlimited Choices" (New York: Reboot, 2006): 23.

[31] Greenberg, "Grande Soy," 24.

[32] Greenberg, "Grande Soy," 26.

[33] Greenberg, "Grande Soy," 27.

[34] Greenberg, "Grande Soy," 25.

The largest, most significant and far-reaching innovations of the past three decades have been the products of an intergenerational partnership in which the grandparents' generation has played a leading role as philanthropists, establishing independent foundations staffed by foundation professionals, who themselves are mainly baby-boomers and Generation Xers, in the service of offering guidance and training to still younger Jews currently in their 20s and 30s. This partnership has fundamentally shaped the character of early 21st century American life.[35]

Wertheimer also proposes that establishment organizations mimic this intergenerational partnership.

Established organizations will have to rethink their governance structures to make room for younger Jewish leaders...Established organizations tend to place younger people on a slower track, testing them and socializing them into the organizational culture before elevating them to positions of influence. This frustrates many creative young people who have experience taking the initiative in other settings and don't want to 'wait their turn.' One can acknowledge the virtues of mentoring and grooming as the preferred way in establishment organizations, while also recognizing that time is not working in favor of those organizations.[36]

Now I will explore some of these "non-establishment" initiatives.

Spotlight on Culture

In 2003, *Time Out New York*'s cover story "The New Super Jew" was the first of many to point out the Jewish cultural revolution. The article said that "edgy young tastemakers are forging a new Jewish identity" portraying a cultural scene in which young Jews are "trailblazing and redefining what it means to be Jewish via 'an explosion' of self-confident, de-institutional, culturally-based organizing from record labels to new forms of synagogue, using festivals, books, and films to build a vibrant Jewish life, created by and for young Jews examining identity, community and meaning on their own terms."[37]

A 2005 *New York Times* article highlighted one of these cultural events:

[35] Wertheimer, "Generations of Change," 4.
[36] Wertheimer, "Generations of Change," 5.
[37] Cohen and Kelman, "The Continuity of Discontinuity," 4.

'A Jewcy Chanukah' is but one of many kitschy celebrations that in the past few years have made comedy as much a part of Chanukah as latkes and sour cream...popping up during what many people have called a Jewish hipster moment...Their humor-laden productions attract thousands of young Jews (some of whom have never gravitated toward their own culture before) and perhaps inadvertently, raise the question of what it means to be Jewish.[38]

In "Grande Soy," Greenberg describes culture as a "convener, communicator and catalyst." Cultural performances and events, "convene an audience that allows for an experience of community," the content of cultural programs "communicates values," and "act as a catalyst for must-have conversation."[39] Today, one can feel Jewish simply by reading a book, commenting on a blog post, watching a Jewish film or attending a Jewish event.

For Elke Reva Sudin, her love of art brought her closer to Judaism:

Why did there have to be a separation between Fine Art and Judaism? This moment of revelation started the process of combining two sides of my personality—the deep spiritual believer and the passionate artist. Suddenly, I started to see Judaism through the lens of the artistic process, and drawing through Judaism.[40]

Just like previous generations have made their mark on American culture through new forms of film and music, this generation is stamping its cultural footprint in innovative art forms and cultural events.

A New Angle on Davening: Independent Minyanim and Post-Denominationalism

In lieu of synagogues, more than 20,000 Jews in their 20s and 30s have connected to the more than 60 independent minyanim that have been launched throughout North America in the last decade.[41] Rabbi Elie Kaunfer, author of *Empowered Judaism* and founder of Kehilat Hadar, one of the first successful models of independent minyanim, says these

---

[38] Stephanie Rosenbloom, "A Happy Hipster Hanukkah," *New York Times*, December 15, 2005.

[39] Greenberg, "Grande Soy," 32.

[40] Elke Reva Sudin, "Juartism," p. 35.

[41] Rabbi Elie Kaunfer, *Empowered Judaism: What Independent Minyanim Can Teach Us about Building Vibrant Jewish Communities*, (Jewish Lights, Vermont 2010): 4.

communities "see themselves as filling a need not being met by existing institutions, but as operating within the larger Jewish community, not outside or against it."[42]

According to Kaunfer, here are the numbers: More than 80% of minyan-goers are under age 40. Of those who attend, 46% grew up at a Conservative synagogue, 20% were raised Orthodox and 18% Reform. Their top two reasons for being involved are to be part of a community and to be part of meaningful prayer.[43] Members of independent minyanim practice "religious traditionalism and social progressivism"[44]—i.e. a minyan that keeps strictly kosher can also be LGBT friendly.

But today, about half of participants do not claim any denominational affiliation, considering themselves "nondenominational."[45] Kaunfer writes, "The more Jews become empowered to define their own Jewish identity, the less likely it is that they will be satisfied by a broad label."[46]

Much research today says denominational affiliation is on the decline—and not just among the younger generation. Wertheimer reports, "Judging from the dramatic shifts in allegiance among younger leaders, especially in the non-establishment category, we may observe that American Judaism is undergoing a significant reconfiguration of denominational identification."[47]

This shift in how young Jews organize and pray is perhaps the most striking divergence from previous generations and reflects a reaction to general cultural shifts in the greater global community.

The Portrait of a Young Jew: Not So Black and White

As much as young Jews today differ from the generations before them, some still feel deeply connected to Jewish tradition, to Israel and even to institutional life. The portrait of a young Jew today is not easily defined, as you will see when you begin to read the collection of essays. As Cohen and Eisen point out in *The Jew Within*, "Quantitative methods

---

[42] Kaunfer, *Empowered Judaism*, 61.

[43] Kaunfer, *Empowered Judaism*, 64.

[44] Steven M. Cohen, J. Shawn Landres, Elie Kaunfer, and Michelle Shain, "Emergent Jewish Communities and their Particiapnts: Preliminary Findings from the 2007 National Spiritual Communities Study" (The S3K Synagogue Studies Institute & Mechon Hadar, 2007): 4.

[45] Kaunfer, *Empowered Judaism*, 64.

[46] Kaunfer, *Empowered Judaism*, 146.

[47] Wertheimer, "Generations of Change," 28.

alone cannot grasp the ways in which contemporary American Jews follow and depart from the attitudes, behaviors and conflicts that they witnessed as children."[48] "What matters...are powerful individual memories and experiences, the personal stories...the personal journeys that they mark and the people who share the most meaningful moments on these journeys with them."[49]

THROUGH THEIR OWN LENS

Living Jewishly: A Snapshot of a Generation, is a collection of personal essays and memoirs from Jewish 20- and 30-somethings from across the country—think Chicken Soup for the Jewish Soul meets Jewcy. My hope is that each piece will be a window into how we express our Judaism and that our voices together will tell a complete story.

Before you continue, here is a guide to some of the common threads and trends I garnered from the essays you are about to read.[50] As you read, you will note that a majority of the essays are written by Jewish professionals or Jewish bloggers—a natural result of a self-selecting submission process. You will notice some overlap with the research above, and some contradiction.

- *Lessons of the past:* Young people often look to the past for guidance and to connect to family and tradition. Many stories—some written by the grandchildren of Holocaust survivors—discuss the influence of grandparents on identity and Jewish practice.
- *Redefining ritual:* Along the same lines, many Jewish 20- and 30-somethings are embracing tradition and ritual while still making it their own—such as Nina Badzin (p. 85), who visits the mikvah regularly but is not otherwise very observant, or Jessica Kirzane, the college student who decides to bake challah each Friday to feel a connection to those who have come before her, though she learned from a recipe book, not from a mother or grandmother (p. 76).
- *The "ish" generation:* This generation does not consider labels to be defining or set in stone, and the lines between the denominations

---

[48] Cohen and Eisen, *The Jew Within*, 3.
[49] Cohen and Eisen, *The Jew Within*, 16.
[50] For a complete index of the essays by subject, see p. 154.

are blurring. Rabbi Jason Miller writes, "As a 30-something rabbi, I've noticed that denominational labels were much more important for our parents' and grandparents' generation than they are for us. Today's 20- and 30-year-olds are searching for meaning in religion and are not very concerned with the names of movements or synagogues" (p. 1).

- *Who is a Jew?:* Many Jews in their 20s and 30s are struggling to make connections, define multiple identities and find personally meaningful community.
- *Dating and relationships:* Young Jews are learning to redefine Jewish relationships in a time of JDate, intermarriage and same-sex marriage.
- *Activism and Jewish professional life:* Members of this generation are concerned about how they will measure up to past generations and be role models for future generations. Ezra Shanken, a Jewish professional, writes "My father registered voters during the Civil Rights movement, marched on Washington, and dug trenches during the Six Day War...Wanting to measure up drives me to be the best Jewish communal professional I can be, while saddling me with a healthy sense of guilt and obligation" (p. 24).
- *Connection to Israel and Hebrew:* Though some research claims young Jews are not as connected to Israel as past generations, some essays reflect a sense of feeling at home in Israel, and a connection to Israel's history and to the Hebrew language, like LynleyShimat Lys who writes of her love affair with Hebrew (p. 22) or Eva Tuschman who finally feels home once she moves to Israel (p. 102).
- *Culture:* Many young Jews are finding Jewish meaning and community through cultural experiences like art, music or blogging.
- *Conflicting values:* Jewish 20- and 30-somethings are learning to navigate the intersection of Judaism and technology, and reconciling Jewish traditions in a modern world.

As you read the essays, I encourage you to challenge these concepts I have outlined—perhaps the picture will appear differently when viewed from your angle.

LIVING JEWISHLY

A Snapshot of a Generation

ARE WE MOVING BEYOND DENOMINATIONAL BORDERS?

By Rabbi Jason A. Miller

AS A 30-SOMETHING RABBI, I'VE NOTICED THAT denominational labels were much more important for our parents' and grandparents' generations than they are for us. Today's 20- and 30-year-olds are searching for meaning in religion and are not very concerned with the names of movements or synagogues.

Rabbi Naftali Rothenberg, an Orthodox rabbi, recently wrote an op-ed in *The New York Jewish Week* entitled "Time To End The Reform-Orthodox Wars." He was responding to Israeli Chief Rabbi Shlomo Amar's attack on Reform Jews and his pressure on the Israeli government to prevent involvement of non-Orthodox movements in state and religion affairs.

I was pleased to read Rothenberg's perspective that it is time for Orthodox Jews to "build bridges of cooperation [to Reform and Conservative Jews] for the sake of the entire people of Israel and its future" without compromising principles or "fidelity to a life of Torah and mitzvoth."

My own sense is that despite some animosity toward other denominations of Judaism, which is often bred on ignorance, there is actually much tolerance and understanding among fellow Jews. We are moving toward a Jewish community in which the borders that separate the denominations are becoming blurred.

1

Rothenberg recognizes the need to bridge the vast abyss between his brand of Orthodoxy and the more progressive streams of modern Judaism, but he remains concerned that the depths of antipathy will make this too difficult. I disagree.

We live in a time when a Jewish person's Facebook profile identifies her religion as "Recon-newel-ortho-conserva-form." This combination of religious denominations does not demonstrate confusion or haziness, but rather the realization that there is "meaning" to be made from the various pathways to Torah.

I knew when I decided to become a rabbi that the Conservative Movement's Jewish Theological Seminary would be the right place for my training. I had been raised in Conservative Judaism, studying at Hillel Day School and honing my leadership skills in United Synagogue Youth, the movement's youth program. However, it was in rabbinical school that I came into contact with the other "flavors" of Judaism—praying each Shabbat at an Orthodox shul, engaging in Torah study with a Reconstructionist rabbi, and training as a hospital chaplain with a Reform rabbinical student.

My first job after graduating rabbinical school was at the University of Michigan Hillel Foundation, an institution that offers five different Shabbat service options. On any given Friday evening I could find myself in a Reform havurah, a Conservative minyan, an egalitarian gathering with separate seating, or a traditional Orthodox service. From week to week, I saw many students sampling the various options, less concerned with ideological labels than with finding a comfort level that spoke to them spiritually, intellectually, and communally. They were in search of meaning, not a denominational brand.

Last year, I traveled to New York City several times to be part of a fellowship with rabbinic colleagues spanning the denominations. We gathered every few months to study Torah together, to pray together, and to dialogue about the important issues of the day. As part of Clal's Rabbis Without Borders program, we found a safe space to share our distinct viewpoints on a host of topics—from faith perspectives on healing to the economy's effect on religion to the role of music in prayer. We might not have all agreed on how the Torah was revealed to the Jewish people in the desert thousands of years ago, but we each managed to share our Jewish wisdom through the medium of Torah.

2

Denominational labels are becoming far less important in the 21st century as the borders have blurred. While I may be a card-carrying Conservative rabbi, I work for Tamarack Camps—a Jewish camping agency that serves the entire community, from the unaffiliated to the religious. I lead a Reconstructionist synagogue, Congregation T'chiyah, in which my more traditional practices and beliefs are not compromised, but respected and admired. I teach teens on Monday nights at Temple Israel, one of the largest Reform congregations in the world. I run a kosher certification business in which I demand the highest levels of kashruth compliance to meet the requirements of our faith and the needs of our community.

Looking beyond the borders that divide our Jewish community is not always easy or comfortable. After all, there are real differences that set us apart. There are always going to be political and ideological conflicts that keep us from praying together or eating together. But we must always seek to dialogue with civility and come together over the issues on which we can agree. A Reform Passover Seder may differ greatly from an Orthodox one, but the context is the same—we are all recalling the days our people spent in slavery. Neither Pharaoh nor Hitler differentiated between Reform, Conservative or Orthodox Jews.

Hailing from Metro Detroit, Rabbi Jason Miller, 34, is a prolific blogger and a "Rabbi Without Borders" who is connected to thousands through Facebook, Twitter, and several blogs. In addition to his own blog (http://blog.rabbijason.com), he is also a blogger for the Huffington Post, *the* New York Jewish Week, *and* CommunityNext. *He is also the founder and director of Kosher Michigan—a kosher certification agency. Currently the year-round rabbi of Tamarack Camps, Rabbi Jason also serves as the part-time rabbi of Congregation T'chiyah, an innovative, progressive synagogue.*

This essay was also published in the Huffington Post, eJewishPhilanthropy *and the* Detroit Jewish News.[51]

---

[51] All contributor bios in this anthology were written in December, 2010.

STARK NAKED OR FULLY DRESSED— WE'RE ALL THE SAME

By Melissa Scholten-Gutierrez

HAVE YOU EVER DREAMT YOU SHOWED UP AT A MAJOR community event stark naked? The reactions range the spectrum from those who stare blatantly and those who attempt to pretend nothing is wrong even though you can tell they are looking at you differently while you go about your evening as if nothing is different. You are certain you appear normal, but feel as though something must clearly be wrong based on the reaction of those around you. It takes some time before you finally realize just what is generating this overwhelmingly uncomfortable reaction to your presence. That is how I feel every time I show up at a Jewish communal event.

I am a proud member of my local Jewish community— in all that it entails. I enjoy social, activist, fundraising, and religious events hosted by a number of fabulous organizations, both small and large. As a vibrant part of the young adult community I feel it is my duty to be present in as many places as possible to show the community at large that we, the upcoming leaders, are not apathetic and do care about the future of the Jewish people and our community. So whether it is a happy hour at a bar, a high-powered luncheon, or anything in between, I do my best to be there to represent my peers.

Given my passion for this, you may wonder why I feel like I am naked. The truth is, I am far from it.

4

As a traditionally observant married woman in a largely secular community I do not blend in. While my modest neckline, elbow length sleeves and calf-length skirts can sometimes pass for a stylish and funky outfit, in a blizzard or on a hot summer's day they definitely do not. However, the single item that always gives me away, and is the ultimate source for feeling like I am naked, is my head covering. No matter how stylishly I tie a scarf or accessorize a hat, I feel like it is a target for the eyes and attention of every person in the room. I have learned that I cannot expect to have a conversation with a person looking me in the eyes (which is something I understood in my college years for very different reasons!) They are either staring at my head covering or trying so hard not to that they avoid any semblance of eye contact.

Over the course of my time in this community, I have learned which events trigger these reactions the most and where I am more apt to find a gentler response. This knowledge will sometimes aid in my decision about whether or not I want to avoid public outings if I do not have a friend to walk in with and serve as a buffer to the "you don't belong here" looks. Regardless of how confident I am in my choice to cover my head and my willingness to speak about it with those who ask politely, some-times I just do not want to deal with the passive aggressive comments, questions, and looks. As much as I love my community, I do not always like having to serve as a token for misplaced anger and misconceptions about the religious contingent of it. I want to be able to attend an event and meet new people and socialize the way I did when my outer appearance matched that of my peers. While we have come a long way in accepting the diversity of our Jewish community, locally and globally, we have a long way to go yet.

I would like to state on behalf of integrated, modern, head-covering women everywhere, we are just like you. If we were not, we would not be at the same events. We are young leaders, activists, and educators, just like you. We are seeking ways to further our involvement in a meaningful way, just like you. In order to allow these commonalities to unite us, rather than our differing religious practices to divide us, I invite you to shift your focus from our hat, scarf, or wig—to us. Take a moment to ask us about the event, what our interest is in the organization, or just about who we are—just as you would any other person. We know how we dress, but we also know who we are; and we would love to show that person to you if you will give us the opportunity.

Melissa Scholten-Gutierrez, 28, is a Federation employee by day, and an educator, writer, and mikvah advocate by night. She is also a future rebbetzin who, in blending her Ashkenazi upbringing with her husband's Sephardic traditions, has coined the term Sephardekenazi. While she has lived many places, Melissa currently resides in Denver, CO.

THE PLAN

By Sharna Marcus

AS A KID, I GREW UP THINKING MY LIFE WOULD TURN out a certain way. At 34, I thought I would be married with three kids, just like my mom and dad. I thought I would have a Jewish husband and we would have couple friends and I'd pick up their kids at soccer practice and they would pick up mine. I'd be teaching at a Jewish day school, to help pay for my kids' tuition there, and my husband would be doing something rewarding, something we would be proud of, but we would live comfortably financially.

And so the day he proposed I viewed it as part of the plan, even though I knew the relationship wouldn't work out. But there he was, on one knee, with the good looks of Prince Charming and the diamond ring I had described to his mom when she asked me my preferences. I was 26 years old. Kid 1 at 29, Kid 2 at 31 and Kid 3 at 33. Perfect.

But the relationship didn't work out, and the damage that it inflicted as well as the baggage I've carried with me has resulted in my life not turning out the way I envisioned, and definitely not the way my mother envisioned.

And as I scour the photographs of my friends on Facebook living the life I always thought that I would live, who choose the salad bar over a conversation with me if I run into them at the grocery store, I wonder if I'm a failure. When I teach at religious school and notice that the parents there are my age, I look at the kids and wonder what mine would have looked like.

It has been argued to me, by my most honest of friends, that I am the lucky one. Husbands grow cantankerous, the sex gets tedious, and kids are really, really hard. I have fallen in and out of love five times since my breakup with my ex-fiancé. I've felt 10 stomachs worth of butterflies before first kisses and several liters of tears after inevitable breakups. I should be thankful that I still feel love, that I still have my freedom. The affliction of marriage and children will come one day.

But for my mother and for me, that answer is unsatisfying. My most recent love said to me, "Your mother has lived her life, you need to live yours."

But it's hard to celebrate a life that does not have a positive precedent or paradigm. Besides the crappy fairy tales, I studied Torah as a kid. There are no single women in the Hebrew Bible who are celebrated (Miriam, maybe? But she doesn't get much air time.) Adam-Eve, Abe-Sara (coincidentally my parents' names), Isaac-Rebecca, and Jacob-Rachel, Leah and concubines. And the first commandment in the Torah is to procreate. The only thing I'm procreating is a clock that is going tick tock tick tock.

However, the societal expectation is that I will be happy with what I have—a great condo, a cute car, a wonderful job, good friends, supportive family—because there are people in the world who are much worse off and no one is going to want to marry me if I have a farbisane punim (sour face).

So I live my life, do my thing, and try not to think about marriage too much and try to get my mother's mind off of it as well. My punim is not farbisana and in general I'm a pleasant person to be around—because why wouldn't I be?

But I won't lie and tell you that I'm living the life that I wanted. But maybe what we want isn't always what we need. And perhaps I don't need the life that I want or that my mother wants for me or the one that all my friends seem to have.

And if you are about to recommend that I try JDate, please punch yourself in the face. Not too hard. We wouldn't want you to give yourself a miskeit punim. God forbid!

> *Sharna Marcus, 35, is the Director of Education at Shorashim and frequently travels between Chicago and Israel. Since she was 18, she has been a journalist, teacher and now director at a not for profit. Sharna is also the co-founder of Makor in Chicago. She grew up in South Bend, Indiana, and has lived in Chicago since 1999.*

SHOMER NEGIAH IN THE CITY

By Matthue Roth

IT WAS THE SUMMER I LEFT SAN FRANCISCO. I'D GOTTEN a book deal, gotten hardcore about this whole Orthodox thing, and hitched a ride with my best friend's ex-girlfriend and her dog to New York City. Suddenly I lived in a city of gorgeous, untouchable Orthodox girls who knew more about Judaism than I even suspected there was to know, who never looked me in the eye, who lived in lavish penthouse apartments in neighborhoods where I couldn't even afford to eat.

Over the course of the summer, I followed Yirmi and Benji, my Jewish socialite friends, to one-dollar drink nights and concerts where they seemed to know everyone and everyone seemed to be Orthodox. Every time I turned around, I caught sight of a guy in a yarmulke. It was like the dream in *Being John Malkovich* where everyone has John Malkovich's face, even the grandmothers and the hot girls in tight dresses. In my case, though, it wasn't the grandmothers and the girls, but jocks and investment bankers in casual Friday khakis. It was half brilliant fantasy—I'm not the only one!—and half nightmare, because even if we had Orthodox Judaism in common, that didn't necessarily mean they were cool people, or even that they had anything interesting to say. In fact, most of them liked to talk about their day jobs. Wasn't this what I moved to New York to get away from?

9

But I needed to go to these lame parties with lame buffets and even lamer MC's. I needed to give up the too-cool game, the too-hip game, the I-don't-need-a-salary-and-health-care-cause-I'm-a-professional-poet game. I needed to do these things because I'd decided that I was Ready To Date.

Admitting to yourself that you are Ready To Date is a pretty big deal among Orthodox Jews because dating is a short step away from getting married, settling down, and pumping out 27,000 babies. It's also a big deal because it means deciding whether or not you're shomer negiah.

Shomer negiah is one of those things that define us as Orthodox Jews, and as human beings. Literally, the words shomer negiah mean "a guard of your touch." If you are a boy, you don't touch girls; and if you're a girl, you don't touch boys. I had just spent the last three years living in San Francisco and not being shomer. To be in New York—with its miles of kosher restaurants and Hasidim who not only knew how to play this game, but actually played it—felt like my ultimate calling. You can play Orthodox Judaism in your backyard, but this was the major league.

Being so out of contact with the mainstream Orthodox world, I didn't realize that there were Orthodox people who followed every law except for that one. Yet my first night in New York, I heard my roommate having his way—loudly, pronouncedly, and at great length—with one (if not two) Hasidic girls in the next room over. I covered my head with a pillow, squeezed my eyes shut, and started humming to myself the Minor Threat song "Straight Edge," which had been my anthem ever since I learned that being a virgin could be a political choice, and that there was a whole punk movement to back me up. But . . . it was out there. And I could have it.

One night, Yirmi and Benji and I were out at another nightclub or meeting or salon of young Jewish professionals and my eyes were glued to the doors, hoping for some big-bearded rabbi to walk in, his coat the color of penguin wings and his eyes like stars, and teach me the real secrets of the universe, why the world rotates east to west and how even shit was part of G-d's creation.

Instead, prerecorded hip-hop samples blasted over a PA system and this short, balding Jewish dude in a gold chain walked in. "What's up, Upper West Side," he crooned into a mic. "Are you ready to parrrrtay?"

We went home that night as an entourage, seven of us to the two-room flat where they lived: me, Yirmi, Benji, and four girls who we'd managed to pick up on the way. At first I pegged them for being recently Orthodox, just like me, because they wore street clothes and didn't talk in Torah talk, but someone said something in Yiddish, and everyone laughed but me. Then I thought they were underage, but someone said that they had their own apartment.

And, like a flash, Benji's arm was around one of the girls and then Yirmi's arms were around two more of the girls and I retreated into my own head, asking myself where I was going and what kind of life was I sinking myself into, and if these were the people I was trying to be like, well then, what were they trying to be like?

I was in my head for barely five minutes, we were less than a block down the street, and already Yirmi was brushing his nose up against one girl's nose, physically parting her lips with his fingers, getting them loose and open and ready to stick his tongue in. A plane soared low overhead. Benji broke free of his girl, threw his arms in the air and spun around and crooned, spontaneously, in the style of that MC from that night: "Are you ready to parrrrtay?"

They were so not ready to party. They were ready to explode, loaded with liquor and energy, and, upon reaching home, they were ready to collapse. Yirmi and Benji and their Hasidic-but-with-a-sex-drive girl-space-friends fell asleep all over the room—on the couches, on the floor, and in their beds. Yirmi, the last one standing, did not seem to mind. He excused himself, slipped under his cover between two girls, one of whom grunted, already half-asleep. The other girl licked his ear.

From his mountain of pillows, eyes half-lidded, he grinned at me. He looked straight at me as the girl licked his ear, as her impossibly long Hasidic tongue slithered around his weirdly straight earlobe, as if it was a private joke between he and I, a joke that I, by virtue of having lived in San Francisco, would immediately understand and appreciate. A look that, if it had been any more loaded, would have been an invitation to an orgy, as if he was asking: Are you down?

And I would have totally gotten down with it, too, back in the old days, between when I decided to be Orthodox and when I decided to take being Orthodox seriously. Now that I was following the rules, what did it mean if the people around me were ignoring them? Was I down? I didn't know.

There was a paradox involved in being openly shomer negiah. If you were shomer, you could date everyone, whether they were shomer negiah or not (although, if one person was and one wasn't, chances were, you were either going to get married or break up pretty fast.) But if you weren't, and you did hook up with girls, then you were off-limits to anyone on the other side of the fence. Untouchable. Dirty. It was like you weren't even Orthodox. Playing the odds, it was better to be shomer negiah. That way, you could date everyone.

It wasn't like I hadn't tried to date when I was in New York. One night, I answered an Internet ad. My friend Jerrica was going over Craigslist, reading the girls-who-like-boys personal ads, which he felt totally giddy and guilt-free about reading, since he was gay. There was one that reminded him of me—Did You Say Modeh Ani Every Morning, And Do You Miss It?—and he double-dared me to answer it.

So I did. And we made plans. We met up at a subway station, jumped on at Times Square, rode to the last stop before Brooklyn. We walked over the bridge, looked down over the water like we were walking directly on it, and followed its spidery descent until we were on a narrow path in the middle of cross-town traffic. She told me her story: she'd grown up Orthodox, the daughter of a rabbi. She'd learned everything forwards and backwards, could speak Yiddish fluently and read a Gemara better than I ever wished I could; but she could never believe any of it. She majored in science, because she said the Torah couldn't agree with science. She moved to this city to get away from her family.

"New York?" I said. "You moved to New York to get away from Jews?"

She laughed. She liked the idea that I replied to her ad, an ad that she was originally afraid would sound too much like a fetish-hunter. I asked her, "What makes you think this isn't a fetish?" She smiled at me like I'd just given her permission for something.

We kept walking. It got late, and we'd managed to walk halfway down the side of Brooklyn, to the front door of her apartment. She hesitated there, and so did I, watching her fidget with the bottom hem of her skirt, which was a few dangerous inches above her knee.

And then her mouth opened, and the question that—like Can I hold that for you? or Want some pizza?—was so rhetorical as to not need an answer, to not even need to be asked, she said to me: "Do you want to come upstairs?"

And, before I knew what the words lined up in my head were, before I could even sort the words in order or realize what they meant, my reply came tumbling out:

"No."

And that was it. We deflated, both of us, into little shriveled-up shards of balloons. We wisped, now no more than stretched-out rubber, having fulfilled our purpose, our usefulness in each other's lives having been outlived, and felt the wind picking up, felt ourselves being blown in opposite directions down the street.

Matthue Roth is 32 years old. He wrote the novel Losers, *the memoir* Yom Kippur a Go-Go, *and the feature film* 1/20, *and is the co-creator of the animated series at G-dcast.com. He's from Philadelphia, lives in Brooklyn and Melbourne, and he really likes praying.*

This essay was originally published on Jewcy.com.

CONVERTED TO REFORM

By Rabbi Julie Pelc Adler

"I'M REFORMED," I HEAR ONE STUDENT TELL ANOTHER by means of explaining his lack of Jewish observance. I cringe, thinking of the years of theological evolution and volumes of critical scholarship underlying the progressive movement of Reform Judaism, none of which inform this young man's Jewish choices.

I remember my own upbringing in the Conservative movement, where I ignored hypocrisies like the rule that girls could not lead services because they were not commanded, as were boys (even though girls *were* allowed to read from the Torah in our synagogue, which hung uncomfortably on the traditional end of the Conservative movement). I spent my Jewish adolescence learning the tradition but dreaming of the forbidden: over and over, I was reminded that becoming a rabbi as a woman was prohibited in the eyes of my mentor. Though my rabbi loved and respected me, he could not encourage me to follow in his footsteps: he could not advocate my becoming a rabbi. Other things were forbidden, too, like cheeseburgers and homosexuality (which my rabbi once mentioned together casually as temptations we must resist). I was a heterosexual vegetarian but the fact of my being female continued to nag at my increasing commitment to and observance of Jewish law.

By the age of 13, I knew I wanted to be a rabbi. Standing on the bimah for the first time, I felt an invisible pull as certain as the light filtering through the stained glass windows casting a rainbow on the plush carpeting beside the holy ark housing the Torah scrolls. There was a certainty to this calling I had never known before: I knew that this was God's wish for me, to become a Jewish leader.

My first year of college, I took Jewish studies alongside Women's studies courses. On school vacations, I returned home and attended services so that I might see my rabbi. By now, I was asking the kind of questions that made him smile (with pride?) and shift uncomfortably in his seat at the same time.

"Why can't women serve as witnesses in the Talmud?"

"How is it ethical to forbid homosexuality if it's not in a person's power to choose to be gay or straight?"

"If the rabbis could find ways to locate loopholes in the text for other things deemed unethical to their modern sensibilities, why not these?"

I now knew that much of the resistance I felt at home was due not to Jewish law, but to politics in the synagogue. I learned the phrase, "where there's a Rabbinic will, there's a halachic way," imploring my home congregation to simply *find* the way.

I initially chose a Conservative rabbinical school, saying that change had to come from within the movement, planning to become a part of that change from within. But by the second year of my studies, the strict observances and rigidity of the Conservative movement began to erode my excitement. My classmates worried aloud whether their homes were kosher enough. I worried I was being swallowed by the rabbinic tradition.

The inconsistencies between my alleged beliefs and the reality of my religious practice flourished as I studied the tradition. I learned how liturgy had evolved over time, shaped by the politics and preferences of each era and I wondered why we did not make more changes to the seemingly unchangeable tradition. I scowled at the refusal to allow openly gay students to enroll in my school and began to say, "If some people are in the closet, then everyone is in the closet."

In the middle of my fourth semester of school, the accumulation of seemingly small compromises made me feel like a liar. Conservative theology had taught me the language of religious obligation, of righteous prayer being rewarded, of walking humbly with God. I walked away. In the spring of 2002, I transferred to the Reform rabbinical school in town, moved away from my predominantly Jewish neighborhood of Pico-

Robertson, and learned to read Tarot cards. I moved to Venice Beach, where I joked that "all the Jews are yoga teachers."

I anticipated the start of a new semester in a new school, but I never said aloud that I was comfortable becoming a Reform rabbi. I imagined myself randomly repeating empty phrases like, "wonderful" and "beautiful," systematically watering down my tradition into bite-sized pieces. I imagined Reform rabbis singing and playing guitars (neither of which I could do); catering to the unaffiliated, disaffected Jews who wanted a stamp saying "kosher" on their ham-and-cheese lives, prioritizing soccer practice over synagogue attendance.

But during that first semester of Reform rabbinical school, I fell in love with my courses, my teachers, and myself. I learned that the holiness of the Torah does not make it immune to modern critique and found that my new teachers saw value in my questions, creativity, and intellectual curiosity. My classmates asked questions about feminist interpretation, and I settled into my skin as a liberal Jew attending a Reform rabbinical school. I pictured the giant wooden doors of the synagogue of my childhood closing before me, leaving me standing forever Outside. My heart ached and laughed.

Julie Pelc Adler, 34, is a Reform rabbi originally from Milwaukee, Wisconsin and currently living in Venice, California with her Conservative rabbi husband, Amitai Adler, and the puppy they rescued from the shelter, Nicky (Pumpernickel) Pelc Adler. She is the Director of Jewish Student Life at Santa Monica College Hillel and the Director of the Berit Mila Program of Reform Judaism. She received master's degrees from the University of Judaism and from Harvard Graduate School of Education and was ordained as a rabbi by Hebrew Union College—Jewish Institute of Religion in 2006. She is co-editor of the anthology, Joining the Sisterhood: Young Jewish Women Write Their Lives, *which was published by the State University of New York Press in 2003.*

ANATOMY OF AN ACTIVIST

By David Levy

IT TOOK A LONG TIME FOR ME TO BE COMFORTABLE calling myself an activist. Although I have been in positions of leadership of some sort or another ever since the fateful night towards the end of the fifth grade when I forgot about Kadima elections and got voted in as the Religious Education Vice President in absentia (when I found out I sobbed), I've always seen a difference between "leadership" and "activism."

When I look back, I can now trace the origin of my career as an activist to one moment, on Shabbat Shuva of 1997. The fall of 1997 began my sophomore year of college. True to form, I had found my way into several leadership positions on campus: I was director of a musical, co-chair of Hillel's Shabbat committee, and one of four gabbaim (organizers) of the Conservative minyan.

A year earlier, I had kicked off my time in college by coming out to my parents. I had set a deadline with myself that I wanted to be out of the closet by the time I started college, and since I'm bad with deadlines, I told them as they were getting back into the car after unloading everything I owned into my dorm room. I imagined that once I told my parents, I would be "out" and it would cease to be a big deal in my life. Of course, that's not how it works, and when half an hour later I found myself in a room full of 40 other new freshmen, I couldn't figure out how to share this newly open piece of my identity, so I kept quiet about it.

Luckily, I happened into a really marvelous group of friends and by the end of first semester I had come out to pretty much everyone I knew at school...except for the Jews. Although there wasn't any antagonism at Hillel, there weren't any signals that it would be okay to be queer in the religious community either. My years of leadership in the Conservative movement had imprinted on me that it wasn't okay to be gay and be a Jewish leader, and since I didn't see anything in college to indicate otherwise, I kept up the double life I had perfected as a USY regional president.

By the time I had become one of the gabbaim of my minyan, I got tired of this bifurcation of my identity. I also had my first wrestling match with an annoying little gnome called Integrity that has continued to harass me throughout my career in the Jewish world. (Don't worry, Integrity and I have since become friends.) And just in case I needed a sign from God (or whoever runs the Jewish calendar) that the issue was coming to a head, National Coming Out Day 1997 coincided with Yom Kippur.

I made up my mind to come out to my Jewish community. I just didn't know how. Being me, I turned to Jewish text. I fixated on a particular section of Pirkei Avot that discusses ethics for interacting with one's community. I wasn't sure when I'd have the opportunity to act on it, but I felt the words of Hillel telling me that in order to remain connected to my community, I could not keep secrets. After all, they'd be heard in the end anyway. And I felt reassured that in the same breath, Hillel cautioned us not to judge, and hoped my community wouldn't judge me.

Once again, I felt the deadline of Yom Kippur/National Coming Out Day looming, and we already know I'm bad with deadlines. However, I knew that Yom Kippur itself would not be an appropriate day for the conversations I needed to have. Luckily, the decision made itself. My minyan had a tradition of learning a piece of mishnah from a different member of the community each week at the end of the service. The Shabbat morning before Yom Kippur, one of the other gabbaim came up to me during the Torah service and "reminded" me that I was on for the mishnah this week. I put "reminded" in quotes because I didn't remember signing up, but I knew this was my chance. After all, Pirkei Avot is mishnah.

Well, you can imagine the rest of the story. The end of the service came, and I got up in front of my community to talk about why I believed that Pirkei Avot required me to come out, and required our community to accept that. Despite being a seasoned public speaker, I was visibly shaking as I stood in front of my friends. And although I did speak about myself,

I focused more on how the calendrical coincidence should make us mindful of how we can ensure that everyone can be a part of our community. I slipped in the bit about which side of the line I stood on so quickly that I could see plenty of faces reflecting the "did I just hear that" spreading through the crowd.

Almost 12 years later, I can still remember every detail of that morning and replay it in slow motion. I remember the awkward silence when I finished speaking, during which the gabbai invited the congregation to rise and say Kaddish d'Rabbanan. I remember sitting back down next to my roommate, who knew I was gay but didn't know I was planning on coming out that morning. I know who spoke to me during kiddush and who sat with me at lunch. It was, in the truest sense of the word, momentous.

Getting up and speaking was an act of activism, but it isn't what made me an activist. What made me an activist is what came next. I continued being a gabbai, I continued co-chairing the Shabbat committee, and I continued all the hundreds of little things I did as part of the Jewish community each week. I can't say that every moment was entirely comfortable, but it was much easier than I imagined, and I became a visible role model to some and a reminder to others. (It was particularly gratifying to me to see that by opening the conversation in this way, others in the Hillel community started talking about gay and lesbian inclusion in our religious communities and planning programs on the theme, even when I wasn't there!) I soon added another position of Jewish leadership to my resume, becoming a co-chair of our Jewish gay, lesbian, bisexual and transgender student group, a position I held longer than any other position of leadership in college. I don't think it's accidental that today, my activism continues to focus on inclusion work in the Jewish community.

And yet, I'm still uncomfortable with the label of "activist." Maybe I'm ashamed that I got tired of coming out—because believe me, even when you're an adult and happy and comfortable with yourself, it still takes energy—and so I often let incorrect assumptions slide. My own first cousins, with whom I'm very close, only recently "figured it out" because they have all joined Facebook this year and saw my pictures from Pride. (I admit, I'm relieved that the pictures did the trick and I didn't have to sit down and have a whole conversation with each of them.) How is it that I can stand up in front of the students and faculty of a rabbinical school and talk about how the policies of the Conservative movement tormented me as a teen, but I can't find the right way to speak about such a huge part of my life to people whom I know love me? I suppose I have nothing to lose when advocating to strangers. (And even though I have never once had someone react badly to my coming out, a lifetime of films and books and plays and news articles about gay kids getting rejected makes me think it's got to happen sooner or later, right?)

Every year I have a new crop of students, and I need to find the right moment come out again to the school. Finding that moment isn't so easy, but I do think it's important. Today, I was having lunch with an old friend in the center of town, and some of my students who just finished seventh grade saw us. They asked me if she was my "soulmate," and when I said no, they kept at it as only pubescent boys can. I told them she's married, and one said to me, "I think you like her anyway." So I turned to him and said, "But I don't date girls," and even though I think of myself as "fully out," I could feel the familiar hollowness in the pit of my stomach while I awaited his response. He froze as the mechanisms of his brain processed the words, and then he walked away, signaling to the rest of his friends that they should too. They were behind me, but I know he had to share the information. I'm not sure what reactions came next, but the kids left me alone for the rest of lunch. Was that an activist moment? I wish it wasn't, but I might be the first gay friend he's ever known. I hope the encounter influenced him for good, but I suspect I'll never know.

And so here I am, a grown-up activist—one who goes to rallies, writes letters to legislators, advocates for change to strangers in synagogues, friends on Facebook, and readers on blogs and on Twitter—and yet still the hardest action is the one-to-one conversation with those closest to me. Going to rallies, writing letters, posting links to articles is easy. Really being an activist means taking risks; like speaking up for your beliefs and being open about who you are even if it might place barriers between you and those you love, those with whom you work, and sometimes those who hold the keys to your own advancement. And no matter how comfortable you get with stating your case, raising funds or rousing rabble, I don't think you can ever really feel comfortable putting yourself out there. But that's a good thing. Because feeling that risk, feeling it in your bones or in your gut, and moving forward anyway is how you know you can really make a difference.

David Levy, 32, is the editor of JewishBoston.com, although when he wrote the essay he was the Associate Director of Prozdor, the High School of Hebrew College. He sits on the board of directors of Keshet, a non-profit working for the full inclusion of GLBT Jews in Jewish life. His undergraduate degree is from Harvard, and he holds two masters degrees from Hebrew College, one in Jewish Studies and one in Jewish Education.

This essay was originally published on Jewschool.com.

HEBREW—A LOVE/HATE RELATIONSHIP

By LynleyShimat Lys

WE'RE NOT BREAKING UP. REALLY. IT'S JUST WHEN YOU move in together. . . you start to notice all those little ways that you're incompatible. I mean, how do I know the difference between *mipne she* and *mishum she* and *mikeivan she* and why can't I just say *because* and have that be the end of it? Why do I have to specify which kind of because or whether it comes before a sentence or a phrase or after a sentence and at the beginning of the next sentence. And why are there so many passive verb forms? You have your *pu'al* and your *pa'ul* and your *hitpa'el* and *huf'al*, and couldn't we just say *was learned* and be done with it?

It's not that I don't love you. We've been together, off and on, for what? Ten years? The alphabet was fine, not a problem . . . well, except for *tav* and *tet*, because no one pronounces the difference, and maybe *khaf*, which is sometimes disguised as *kaf* and sometimes as *haf*, which sounds like *het*, and then I get confused between *tahanat cafe* and *tachanat cafe,* or maybe it's just that *coffee station* sounds more poetic than *coffee grinder*. So the letters are ok . . . except when *heh* sounds like *aleph*, or like nothing at all when it disappears into a vowel. But we'll get past that.

It's hard when every time I use a verb, I have to think whether it's a verb that takes a *from* or an *in* or an *in the*

22

face of, or *on*, or *towards*, or *over*. In Russian I could just add a prefix to the verb and it would mean *across* or *over*, like *prospala* (I overslept). But no, no prefixes, just roots that take seven verb forms and then infinitives, and verbal nouns and adjectives. Some things are easier in Arabic—no infinitives, for example, just verbal nouns, *doing, seeing, being*. . . why do we need *to see* and *seeing*, *to look* and *looking*, *to be* and *being*? Ok, so English has both. And Arabic has nine verbal forms and case endings, *I, me, to me, of me*, and Russian has six cases. But Hebrew uses *be, in* for the instrumental case—I wrote *with* a pen, *using* a pen.

And yes, unlike Polish, you don't have a vocative case, rather a word, *harei, we all know, hinei, here is*, yes, that works in your favor. You don't see me moving in with Polish. Too many verb conjugations, too many cases. Too conservative. Even Russian drops some words and changes over time. You do have verbs of aspect, like the Slavic languages. Completed action and ongoing action. I lived with you, I was living with you, I live with you, I am living with you, I will live with you, I will be living with you.

Your causatives, derived from the same root as reflexives and actives and passives. One root, many meanings. You're messing up my head with roots and structures and verbs. And expressions! Expressions of time, and causes and reasons and goals. And little words to connect them all. So many little words. Every sentence full of little words that stand alone or stick to something. Some of them stick to me. They push and pull me. Toward and over and under and through, in and on and up over. As if it isn't enough that you've moved in and you accompany me everywhere, your little words are on the ceiling and in the refrigerator, on the couch, through the window. . . everywhere!

LynleyShimat Lys, 33, is a poet, playwright and essayist living in Jerusalem and studying for an MA in Middle Eastern Studies at the Hebrew University. She studied Yiddish film and worked in education at Park Avenue Synagogue in New York before making aliyah in September 2009.

DOES BEING A JEWISH YOUNG PROFESSIONAL TODAY MEAN NEVER MEASURING UP?

By Ezra Shanken

THERE IS A QUOTE IN PIRKEI AVOT (THE ETHICS OF our fathers): "Who is happy? He who is content/happy/satisfied with his lot." Yeah right! This is 2010 and in our young Jewish world the statement should read: "Who is happy? He who has a lot that their friends, family and coworkers covet and admire." Lot could include everything from career and education, to what car we drive or house we live in. No matter what it refers to, I have found that most of us are guilty of coveting each others' lots. Thus, I ask you: Does being a Jewish young professional in the 21st century mean never measuring up?

As an active young Jewish professional, I have the opportunity to attend many events in my day-to-day life. One of the things I find humorous is to see the first questions that people ask each other when they meet, after "what is your name." I find that the next question is not very often "how do you connect spiritually?" or "what are you passionate about?" It is more likely "what do you do?" Now don't get me wrong—I am just as guilty of this, but it is very telling about our generation that this is the first thing we want to know about a person after their name. We are unconsciously starting to paint a picture of who a person is by what they have accomplished. Also, when people answer, they are not telling us what they do as a volunteer or what they do that brings them real joy—they tell us what they do to bring home the kosher turkey bacon.

You are what you do. And what you do right now is never as good as what you could be doing. If you are a medical student you are not a doctor; and if you are a doctor you are not a surgeon; and if you are a surgeon you are not a brain surgeon. This brings me back to our original question: Does being a Jewish young professional in the 21st century mean never measuring up? So far my answer is a resounding maybe.

I was recently watching the movie *The Social Network* about the founding of Facebook and was struck by the opening scene: Mark Zuckerberg is talking to his then girlfriend about how he needs to do something great so that he can be accepted into a private club at Harvard. What is the project he ends up doing? Facebook! Here is a guy that is already at Harvard, yet can't even live in the moment of being there because he is already moving on to the next big thing. Talk about not feeling like you measure up. However, it is the lack of measuring up that pushed him to create Facebook, make a billion dollars and give 100 million dollars away to the Newark public school district. This drives me to a new question: Is it bad that being a Jewish young professional in the 21st century means never measuring up? Maybe not for the Newark public school district.

Now, the idea of not measuring up is also a very personal concept for me. Being a third generation Jewish communal professional, I live with the constant need to not only measure up but surpass the generations that came before me—though I fear that may not be happening anytime soon. My father registered voters during the civil rights movement, marched on Washington, saw the "I Have a Dream" speech and dug trenches during the Six-Day War, not to mention being part of some of the first groups to actively protest the need for inclusion of women in the Conservative rabbinate. Meanwhile, my grandfather has forgotten things he has done that are more significant than that—and he is a rabbi. Wanting to measure up drives me to be the best Jewish communal professional I can be, while saddling me with a healthy dose of guilt and obligation. I show up early and stay late. I am everywhere I can be, and want to be anywhere I can't. I have happily committed myself to a life of no boundaries between where I am what I do no matter where I go.

My final question is this: Is the fear of not measuring up the greatest motivator that we have?

Is the fear like rocket fuel, and our decision is which direction to point the rocket? Do we point it down to a life of materialism and greed where our accomplishments are measured purely by the things we have not acquired; or up to a life where we can be happy with the lot that we have and the people we truly are? Maybe what we are constantly trying to measure up to is a life that needs no measurement.

Ezra S. Shanken, 30, is a third generation Jewish communal professional presently serving as the director, Emerging Leaders and Philanthropists at UJA Federation of New York. Previously, he was the Senior Manager of the Young Adult Department and Major Gifts at the Allied Jewish Federation of Colorado and is co-founder of E-3 Events which brings arts based social program to young Jewish professionals in Colorado. Ezra is a board member of both Ramah of the Rockies and The Mizel Jewish Museum and lives in Denver, CO.

CARD CARRYING MEMBER

By Abby Sher

I'VE ALWAYS WANTED TO BELONG.

To the Girl Scouts. The band. The cool kids who wore CB ski jackets and made out by the gazebo. In college it was the improv troupe, the choir, sometimes Hillel House. More often, the cool kids who drank wine coolers and espresso and tried to reinvent Plato by the bike racks. After graduation, I joined another theater, got a membership to a gym, my own account at Blockbuster, First Chicago Bank. To this day, I get a thrill from flipping open my wallet to reveal my bright green library card, my insurance card, my ten-cups-of-coffee-and-the-eleventh-is-on-us card. I treasure and maybe idealize the notion that there is a greater whole, a group of doctors or books or cups of coffee that know me, care about me, count me as one of their flock.

So it's embarrassing to admit that I have not belonged to a temple since 1991. That's when I moved from West-chester, New York, to start at University of Chicago. We had a family membership at Larchmont Temple, the Reform synagogue in my town where my mom helped found the nursery school and I was bat mitzvahed. I never made an active choice to apply—I was just brought in and accepted. But once I moved to the Midwest, I became a Jewish drifter, catching the Shehechyanu here and a Dayeinu there. Every once in a while dropping off some canned yams for a yearly food drive or writing a check for $36 around Rosh Hashanah, but really living and worshipping off the kindness of strangers.

In Hyde Park, I used my student status as an excuse. I went to the campus synagogue now and then, mostly treating it like another language class since the prayer books had a lot more Hebrew than the one I'd grown up with. My first job out of college was up in Evanston, so I snuck into a local shul there and found a new twinge of delight from being completely anonymous. Walking outside on a breezy Yom Kippur afternoon, I remember feeling energized by my solitude, and yet still connected by a minor chord that everyone was singing. Together.

I joined the Second City family in the late 90s, and the beautiful, generous producer emeritus Joyce Sloane took me under her wing for the High Holidays. She often wears large wool shawls and she literally tucked me in to her warm bosom as we sat next to each other at Anshe Emet in Wrigleyville. She insisted I nap on her day bed before we returned for Neilah services.

I moved back to New York in 2004, just days before my mother died. My father had passed away years before, my siblings had settled in other towns so our family status at Larchmont Temple was extinct. I moved in with my raised-Catholic-but-now-toying-with-atheism boyfriend in Brooklyn, feeling achingly adrift. I joined a yoga studio. I collected more of those coffee cards. I got a monthly metrocard and made sure I used one train for all my commuting needs even if it meant walking a half-hour across town to get to my temp job. I avoided temple for most of the year, then usually found my way to a cousin's Seder or a friend's break the fast. Whenever I crept into the back row of a new synagogue, I made sure to leave without exchanging any hellos or making eye contact with the clergy.

Sure, there's been a financial aspect to my drifter status. How can I commit to annual dues when I don't know how often I'll get to services and don't even know what they serve at oneg? There's also the pull to be anonymous again, to ride on that sea of voices, maybe even allowing me to join in louder because—hey, these people don't know me. And there's sheer laziness. Every Rosh Hashanah I slip into a different folding chair and then promise myself this time I'm going to stay. I'm also going to read Thomas Friedman's *From Beirut to Jerusalem* and keep up with the general elections and/or bake chicken on Friday nights. None of which I've come close to doing since I left Westchester in 1991.

Which brings me back to Larchmont Temple. This year, the Tuesday before Yom Kippur I emailed my rabbi from childhood. I know it's last minute, but any chance you'd have an empty seat if I promise to stay awake for the sermon? He wrote back immediately: Of course. Would love to see your punim. Ticket will be by the Willow Street entrance, where you used to creep in late to Hebrew School.

Though the sanctuary has been renovated and most of the members were new to me, I wept gratefully, hearing the familiar chords from the piano, gazing at the white embroidered Torah covers, the sun catching in the same stained glass I'd seen for my first 18 years of life. It was just as warm and soothing as I'd remembered it. I saw many of my parents' friends, some now toting grandchildren. I tried to pick out who was there from my Hebrew school class and whether they were here just for a visit? To live here more permanently? Or maybe somewhere in between...

My rabbi spoke about Zionism and Judaism and how the newest generation of young adult Jews—the campers and confirmation classes he instructs—have no concept of Israel as their home. I can't say that I do either. Friedman still sits on my shelf. I catch bits and pieces of the current peace talks in the news and struggle with how to trace it back to Israel's birth 62 years ago. I listened to my rabbi and now good friend describe essentially me—an adolescent in grown up clothes, still unsure of what and where constitutes my Jewish home.

So this is my New Year's Resolution numero alef for 5771. I am going to join a congregation this year. It could be Larchmont Temple, though I think the commute from Brooklyn would be hard with two kids in diapers. More likely it will be one of the doors I've walked through in Ft. Greene—my neighborhood for the past six and a half years and hopefully for many more. Maybe it will be Union Temple, where Rabbi Goodman's words have challenged me to think about my role in health care reform. Or the Brooklyn Jews' congregation led by Marc Katz and Jennifer Gubitz, who've welcomed me at Rosh Hashanah in the picnic house at Prospect Park, even inviting me onto the bima to be part of an aliyah for new mothers. Or maybe it will be somewhere I've never been to before. Where I am an anonymous voice, singing loudly. And I return. I say hello, and thank you. I commit to sharing in this sacred spiritual practice.

Abby Sher is a writer and performer living in Brooklyn, New York. She hails from Larchmont, New York, and once snuck out of Hebrew School to eat a ham and salami sandwich. Her memoir, Amen, Amen, Amen: Memoir of a Girl Who Couldn't Stop Praying *was published by Scribner in October, 2009. It got a nod from Oprah and won ELLE Readers' Prize, Chicago Tribune's Best of 2009, and Moment Magazine's Emerging Writers Award. Abby also wrote a young adult novel, Kissing Snowflakes, which is about first kisses and stepmoms. Her words are in* Modern Love: Tales of Love and Obsession, Behind the Bedroom Door, The New York Times, The L.A. Times, Self, Jane, Elle, Elle UK, Marie Claire, HeeB, *and* Redbook.

This essay was originally published on Oy!Chicago (www.oychicago.com).

MY JEWISH JOURNEY: HOW BEING CATHOLIC HELPED MAKE ME JEWISH

By Brian M. Judd

BY MY THIRD DAY OF KINDERGARTEN, I HAD MASTERED the art of saying goodbye to my mom without crying and began enjoying the independence of half-day school. I had my desk, knew my neighbors, and had my bearings. This wasn't going to be so bad after all. And the best part was that it was this pretty Catholic school across the street from a huge, cool church.

Just when I thought I had everything figured out, my teacher began talking about this guy named Jesus who sounded pretty cool: the son of God, made lots of food out of nothing, and was telling people to be nice to each other. She then told us that he died on a cross for us, to save our souls from perpetual torture, and to make us free. Fear struck my heart, panic filled my body, and I ran out of the room with the teacher's aide chasing me close behind. I crumpled to the floor sobbing, confused about this death and convinced that my classmates and I all had to die, to thank Jesus for what he did. The TA comforted me, laughing, not sure how I got this notion in my head. As she laughed, I was trying to figure out how there were eight other grades filled with students. Were they all transfer students and did no one wonder what happened to all of the kindergarteners in this ritual sacrifice?

31

This initial exposure to the story of Jesus defines my relationship with Catholicism: confusing, scary, and a little funny. The beginning of the end; with these first steps, it's no wonder I became a Jew.

I was born the son of an Irish immigrant mother. She came to the United States at 16 to enter the sisterhood. She was a Catholic nun for 10 years, until deciding to leave and have a family outside of the religious order. A few years later, she met my father: a Southern Baptist, Korean War veteran from Texas. They married, formed a Catholic home and had my brother, a heterosexual who became an Evangelical Christian, and me, a gay man, who became Jewish.

My struggle with Catholicism was life-long, although I did not have an experience like the one often depicted in exploitation movies. The schools I attended were primarily private schools, with a religion class and occasional religious services. I took years of religious education and the only elements I internalized were living your life in service and striving for social justice. The rest went in one ear and out the other.

When I turned 14, my parents empowered me to engage with the Church on my own terms. So, I stopped attending church outside of school services. It was around this time that I also read *The Chosen* for a class. I found this world described by Chaim Potok both puzzling and intriguing. Something about the rituals and lives these people led stirred something in me. I felt strangely connected to Judaism. It seemed like a purer form of spirituality than the separated, hierarchical structure I was exposed to; a back-to-basic monotheism, if you will. I essentially played out Jewish values while engaged in Catholicism, via community service, leadership, and community building. I helped lead retreats under the banner of the high school campus ministry program, but did not give one care about Jesus and whether (H)he was present or not. Nothing against the guy, but his followers creeped me out and I thought they got in the way of the true spirituality that arises when people form bonds with one another while striving for community and social justice.

As a college student, I tried to engage in the campus ministry program, but my emerging gay identity and complete disinterest in the Church sucked all the love I had for any of this community work. I then jumped head first into Jesuit-inspired skepticism about everything. I had a short-lived atheist, everything-means-nothing phase, interrupted by this nagging feeling that there was, indeed, something bigger than myself at play in the world.

When I started dating men, I was drawn to one particular type: Jew! No goyim for me, even when I was one! I found my beshert. Michael and I met via a gay men's social group. We connected immediately and have been together for 10 years.

Michael and I moved in together and created a Jewish home. I had long abandoned any Catholic practices, complete with rejecting Christmas decorations, much to his delight. I had no problem with existing in a Jewish home, but was not sure if I wanted to be Jewish myself. We sought out a religious community that would meet Michael's level of observance and would welcome me as a non-Jewish partner. No easy feat. After months of searching, we became founding members of a progressive synagogue called Kol HaNeshamah. Concurrently, Canada legalized same-sex marriage, and we married in Michael's parents' home in Vancouver, British Columbia. We received the first auf ruf in our synagogue's history.

Shortly after, I approached our rabbi about converting to Judaism. I took the intro classes and it was all interesting and wonderful. But, I did not want to be a second class citizen under a different paradigm. I did not see how I would fit into anything but Reform Judaism, and I had little interest in being accepting in only one slice of Jewish life. I backed away from conversion for a bit, to take space and learn more about how queer Jews exist in Judaism at-large. Two years later, on Yom Kippur, I decided that I would make the final decision whether or not to convert. I did not want to disrespect my community by sitting on the fence and remaining ambivalent.

Looking back, Judaism called after me all along. I struggled with the idea of converting, however, because I wasn't sure if I would ever truly be accepted by Jews at-large. I then met a man who would become a dear friend and great influence in my life, in the form of a Chasidic rabbi. I found a few of his sermons/lectures on iTunes and was energized by his words and perspective on Torah. He found a way to be both Chasidic and open to existing in the general world.

When I met the Rabbi, one of the first things he asked me was if Michael and I were going to have children. "If you become Jewish, it will be a double-mitzvah. Get to it!" I sat stunned—an Orthodox rabbi was pressuring me and my gay husband to have children. It was then I realized that I would never be a second class citizen in Judaism. If he could exist in the Orthodox community and treat me as such an equal, then I could be a Jew. There might be individuals or groups that reject me, but if I need a place at a Shabbat table, want to study Torah, lay tefillin, or join a minyan, I would be considered a Jew. Period.

That was all I needed; I completed my conversion studies. Six months later, I went to mikvah and officially became a Jew. Since then, I have co-chaired a rabbinic search process for my synagogue, I am currently the Chair of Religious Life, attend shul regularly, am engaged in the Jewish community at-large, traveled to Israel, and proudly identify as a Jew.

My moment of Jesus-related trauma in kindergarten foreshadowed my relationship with Catholicism, but without the Church I would have never been prepared to become Jewish. The Catholic values of service, social justice, and community were easily transferable to Judaism. Unfortunately, as I saw it, Catholicism prepares one to die; Judaism teaches one how to live. Becoming Jewish was less about finding a home and more about coming home, to a place that was familiar, comfortable, and just right. I found a community where the struggle was part of the experience, an essential part of living life and growing spiritually.

Brian Judd has called Seattle, Washington home for the most part of his 33 years, where he shares his home and life with his husband of six years. Brian works as a Community Center Director for Seattle Parks and Recreation and is a cinephile, with passion spanning from Stanley Kubrick to the French New Wave to American Independent films. When asked by an Israeli customs agent what his favorite Jewish holiday was, he gained easy access to the homeland by truthfully replying, "Passover."

JUARTISM

By Elke Reva Sudin

IN THE FALL OF 2005 I LEFT MY HOMETOWN OF Longmeadow, Massachusetts for Pratt Institute, an art school in Brooklyn, New York. I set out to study illustration, and the last thing on my mind was finding a Jewish community to give me a guilt trip. After many combative years in Jewish private schools, I had switched to a local public school to get my artist's portfolio together as a high school senior. In college I was just going to be me; wherever I would find myself is where I would be.

I started classes. Each lit up my mind in a different way. For my foundation drawing course, the fundamental basis of the creative process, I had Professor Sayler. Sayler had a reputation for being difficult and pushing his students. My placement in his section was seemingly random, but I immediately connected to his approach of "Transformationalism," an almost existential ideology. His lessons taught realistic rendering by developing awareness without the distortion of our minds' filters. We learned to draw objects how they were, not how our mind thinks they appear. He taught how to live in the present—experiencing life moment by moment, and paying attention to the details our senses pick up. He taught us each breath should be significant, each mark of charcoal deliberate, focused, and accurate. Drawing takes a lot of practice, but it's like riding a bike—once you learn how you can go anywhere. This was the place where I really got it.

Photo credit: David Zimand

35

Not neglecting my tradition completely I found the on-campus rabbi and attended my first "Kabbalah and Sushi" lunch with Rabbi Simcha Weinstein and the few committed Jews at Pratt who showed up. Weekly lunch meetings were followed by Friday night Shabbat dinners, in the boisterous spirit befitting an art-school student group. Rabbi Simcha used humor and pop culture references tossed with terms like "kabbalah" and "chassidus" in a way I never heard before. He used these as launching points to describe an outlook on life that was transcendental, citing that these ideas actually come from the Torah and our tradition. To me, it was a radical way of looking at the world, in line with what I was experiencing in art school. It was like the inmates finally ruled the asylum—an open, artistic viewpoint was a common understanding, and that the outside world was now the one considered foreign, weird, and different.

I investigated more with classes at the Chabad of Midtown where Rabbi Shlomo Yaffe, a master scholar of secular and Judaic academics, taught Tanya. My mind moved back and forth between Professor Sayler's teachings and this different way of looking at Judaism, and a question started to percolate. Why did there have to be a separation between Fine Art and Judaism? This moment of revelation started the process of combining two sides of my personality—the deep spiritual believer and the passionate artist.

Suddenly, I started to see Judaism through the lens of the artistic process, and drawing through Judaism. Drawing, like Torah study, can be understood on different levels, from its simplest interpretation, all the way to esoteric interpretations. The seemingly arbitrary mark or method presents itself in true clarity. There is reasoning behind color theory—how colors relate to each other like musical notes, and how we relate to their individual vibrations. Mitzvot reflect the way we as people relate to our surroundings. Some aspects we have lost touch with and lose relevance, others deal with new circumstances and we devise ways to adapt. Art is the language for creative problem solving on a level that our intellect and soul responds to. Our intellect judges design. When performing life-drawing (drawing from observation rather than copying a flat image) we use intellect to access the object. A (spiritual) trained hand guides the drawing implement over paper, careful yet with confidence. A stroke of elegance that is a perfect expression of the outer physical characteristics and of the subjects' inner qualities, bringing life, story, and Torah ideology to a mark on paper.

Rosh Hashanah came. It was my first away from home, ever. This was my first meaningful Rosh Hashanah in my whole life, and I soon learned I was not alone. At the same time, in the same synagogue, another Pratt student was having a very connected experience through art and Judaism. His name was Saul Sudin. Over Friday night dinners at Rabbi Simcha's apartment we struck up conversations, discussing music, classes, commentary, and past experiences. A shared recognition of similar appreciations started to form. Although stylistically very different, we forged what would become the foundation of our friendship and eventually lead into stronger views on art, Judaism, and each other.

It is now five years later and Saul and I have been married for three of those. We still go to that same synagogue where we spent that first Rosh Hashanah. Over that time I ended up being the president of the Pratt Jewish student union for two years, created numerous projects in school including illustrations of World Boxing Association Champion Yuri Foreman and an illustrated book which later turned into a painting series called "Hipsters and Hassids." H&H is to date the most specific form of merging art and Judaism, comparing the dominating cultures in Williamsburg, Brooklyn who may seem to be completely different from one another, but in fact have many parallels.

My artistic and Judaic characteristics melded so deeply that it became difficult to decipher one from the other. I started reaching out to other Jews in the arts and eventually joined the board of the Jewish Art Salon based in Manhattan. I stayed connected to the Pratt Jewish student group that served me well and joined Saul as he established the Jewish Alumni Association of Pratt Institute. More and more I connected to other creative Jews, which lead me to curate art shows for the Jewish diversity organization Be'Chol Lashon, music label Shemspeed, and volunteer with Artists 4 Israel.

Though both committed to our artistic endeavors, Saul and I felt there was a lack of understanding for our craft both in the greater Jewish community, and in the greater art-world. We saw a need for a place for contemporary Jewish artists to be appreciated in a unified global community. Enough division—that's the talk of the 20th century. The 21st century is about having the pride to fight against cultural ignorance. We are unapologetic about our Judaism.

The idea came about to start an anthology publication showcasing contemporary Jewish artists who do really interesting work—a central place for all our new connections. We could design it, get it printed, get people involved online. We thought, "Why not? We have the technology!"

Once the seed was planted, I ran. No looking back. It was going to be now, while it was new, while the idea was fresh and exciting. If I was ever going to be able to sustain the concept of a Jewish approach to art and an artistic approach to Judaism it had to be in a non-discriminating environment. It had to be a product that was meaningful both to Jews and non-Jews, and all art-minded individuals.

Now *SUDINmagazine* is taking off with our first issue, a print edition that showcases some of the most amazing artists and designers we know, complimented by JewishArtNow.com, a website that hosts Jewish art news, exhibitions, and resources. We look forward to facilitating Jewish art programming across the U.S. and abroad as well as providing a platform for new Jewish artists to have their work shown, networked, and appreciated.

With *SUDINmagazine* we aim to make these connections for other people. We present Jewish unity through art in the developing creative process format. No shtick, no kitsch. True to the arts, and true to Judaism (whatever that means!). We are proud of both.

As an artist I have a great responsibility. I am endowed with the powers created in God's image to create for myself. To illustrate an idea, to create a new world-view for someone else, or for others to share some insight into my perspective. Expression of the soul and trigger of intellect drive the creative process. The most rewarding moments come out of creative problem-solving.

Jewish artists or artists who deal with Judaic themes have many different ways to communicate, because there are so many dialogues to explore. For me, I consider my artistic process Jewish. The process includes laying out a design, designing a composition, creating balance, representing subjects to be recognizable, balance and structure, utilizing mark, weight volume, juxtaposition, techniques to describe space and an understanding or communication of a concept or situation. This process is what makes me a Jewish artist. I take responsibility for the outcome because it's my way of serving God. The sketchbook is my commentary/ Talmud, always an exploration. For many Jews this is a puzzling matter thatthey never have to consider. But to me it's the life I live and the gift I hope to give to others.

Elke Reva Sudin, 23, the founder and executive director of SUDINmagazine, *is an illustrator redefining art for the 21st century Jewish community. Sudin, who created the "Hipsters and Hassids" painting series, was recently named the Art Director of* PresenTense *magazine. Her work has been collected at the Museum of Modern Art (MOMA) in New York, and has been featured in publications including the* New York Press, Jewish Week, ZEEK, *and* Tablet Magazine. *She lives with her filmmaker husband, Saul, in Brooklyn.*

NOT YOUR GRANDFATHER'S MINYAN (ALTHOUGH HE MIGHT BE THERE TOO)

By Jeremy Lite

ACCORDING TO A REPORT BY THE UNITED JEWISH Communities and the Jewish Federations of North America, 34% of all synagogue members between the ages of 18-34 belong to an Orthodox synagogue. Among all "young" Jews (those 18-39), 11% identify as Orthodox. It is no surprise that growing numbers of communities are drawing younger Jews to daven in the mornings before going about their varied days. And the under-40 contingent makes up the majority in a growing number of cases! This is not just in New York. This is not just among yeshiva and rabbinical students. It is a nationwide trend, drawing a diversity of observant Jews together for shacharis just after dawn, and again in the evenings for maariv, no matter where they live.

The growing youthfulness of many daily minyans may reflect a general trend toward greater connection and observance. In 2006, Samuel C. Heilman wrote an entire book about this phenomenon among the Orthodox, *Sliding to the Right: The Contest for the Future of American Jewish Orthodoxy* (University of California Press). In his treatment of Orthodoxy, he observes in his introduction that:

The Orthodox . . . manage to do something that few other Jews achieve: they change the communities into which they have moved rather than becoming changed by them. Thus, because they will not acquiesce to a diminished level of Jewish life, no matter where they live, the entry of Orthodox Jews into small Jewish communities has frequently promoted greater religious and ethnic participation in these places.

Simply put: American Orthodox Jews have been able to make Jewish life in such communities flourish.

For many observant Jews in my Arizona town, no matter what our background, we intersect in the mornings for a diverse minyan of professionals, students, educators, and more. And from there we disperse. It is our daily diaspora. Luckily, we can't get too far in a day, so we come back together for mincha and maariv. What happens in between? For me, it is the challenge to weave observance into daily professional life.

I go to court over toxic torts, liquor licenses, and hazardous waste. I respond to fuel spills and manage water rights conveyances. Most of the time, I interact with straightforward, creative, right-minded people. All too often, though, I sit across from difficult, angry, self-interested people. Such is the nature of the business. As a relatively new partner in a small office of a national law firm, my days between shacharis and mincha/maariv are fun, hectic, challenging, and threateningly secular. And that is where the real battle lies.

The challenge of weaving Torah and mitzvah observance into fast-paced, pressure-filled days in a national business law firm is no small task. Searching for holiness while hearing people lie in court is a tough assignment. Setting a time to learn every day is essential. Checking in on COLlive.com and reading Chayenu are important correctives. Remembering to say the right brachas goes without saying. The imperative to judge others favorably is not only a requirement, it is also a helpful coping mechanism. Refraining from harmful speech is a commitment under frequent assault. Keeping shabbos is obviously not negotiable.

Rising above requires staying within—going up, not out. And it requires a long-term vision, including a commitment to building community and supporting our shuls and Jewish institutions. Most cities have a Jewish Community Foundation—Southern Arizona has a particularly strong one. Just as our daily minyans are growing younger, so, too, the task of perpetuating Jewish learning and community must also shift to us. As we read every morning after Shema, "Upon the earlier and the later generations, this affirmation is good and enduring forever."

Right now, as adults aged 20 to 40, we are the latest of the later generations able to take on leadership roles. The more members of our generation that participate willingly, joyfully in this daily event—which our employers will accept and our children will see—the more we will come to internalize the essential nature of our mission. And the more we will carry it forward into our professional lives and communities.

Jeremy Lite, 40, lives in Tucson, Arizona, though he was actually born in Tehran, Iran to a U.S. diplomat father and bounced around a bit before ending up in Tucson. He is a partner in the Tucson office of the Milwaukee- and Chicago-based law firm of Quarles & Brady LLP. He also presently chairs the Project Dor Habah (Next Generation) Committee of the Jewish Community Foundation of Southern Arizona. Since his first visit to Israel coincided with the first Indiana Jones *movie (*Raiders of the Lost Ark*), he came back wanting to be an archaeologist—which he eventually did for five years with an anthropology degree from Michigan before changing course and going to law school in Arizona.*

THE BEGINNER

By Tamara Mann

WATERMELON, WATERMELON, ERMELON, WATERMELL
...lon. The front row girls told me if I said watermelon really quickly I would blend into the morning prayers despite my Hebrew deficiencies. So that's what I did. It was my first day at a yeshiva high school and I desperately wanted to go unnoticed. All that summer I had one persistent dream: I wake up, eat my breakfast, walk to school, enter the morning prayers and then, only after an ear shattering squeal from the boys section, do I realize that I am completely naked. To compensate, I dressed for my first day in layers. My underwear, leggings, socks, t-shirt, cardigan and ankle length skirt made me look like an overstuffed potato. But, I thought, at least I look like an Orthodox overstuffed potato.

When I turned 11, I decided to rebel in the absolute safest manner by becoming an Orthodox Jew. I lorded over the home in months of self-righteous glory by koshering the kitchen and putting sticky notes next to lights that had to stay on throughout Shabbat. My parents, with the kind of patience I have yet to cultivate, simply supported me. They let me transfer to a yeshiva high school, spend all of my summers with an Orthodox family in Israel, and pretty much throw our family habits into disarray. And then, when they finally found a few Orthodox friends and felt welcome in the community, I was over it. I chose a college without an Orthodox community and proceeded to become, in my father's sensitive estimation, "completely whacked out."

I studied contemporary performance art, radical politics, critical theory, and any German philosophy I could get my hands on. I wrote my senior thesis on Theodor Adorno's theory of autonomous art. And then, when my folks finally thought I would settle down and become the trial lawyer they raised me to be, I eschewed the LSATs for a master's degree in World Religion. I spent the next three years of my life studying comparative religion and working with immigrant religious groups in New York City.

I knew how to play faithful. I knew how to dress, tilt my head, cross my legs, and nod at the appropriate moments to endear religious authorities to me. But, perhaps more importantly, I empathized with their ability to subordinate individual whim for the benefit of community. For this reason, I could listen to their fears rather than their rhetoric. And their fear, I soon realized, was always the same: failing to transmit their tradition to their children and grandchildren.

I both admired and resented their ardor to preserve. I constantly had the feeling that I had betrayed them. By living this peculiar life between faiths I had somehow abandoned my own. And, to make things more complicated I had a secret. For three years, I had been dating a *goyisha* man I met in college. I remember sitting at the United Nations with a Rabbi, an Imam and a Bishop and simply lying about my love life. I didn't owe them anything. They weren't family members. And yet, I couldn't come clean. I couldn't admit that my daily choices were so completely at odds with ideals I admired but failed to articulate.

Despite my conflicting set of life choices, I had always conducted a love affair with Judaism. For me, life made sense in my uncle's dining room at Pesach, when I could be a part of my family's cacophony of arguments, melodies, and table banging. Exhausted from my daily life of moderate hypocrisy, I left the Interfaith Center and the study of world religion. I took a job in Jewish education and embarked on a joint journey with my now-husband Ben toward conversion.

I entered a world of cozy familiarity. During the day, I worked with Jewish teachers and at nights I attended introductory classes on Judaism. I cherished the complete lack of stress that came from being a beginner surrounded by other beginners. Without expectations, we each engaged in the conversation with an earnest calm.

The class gave me the confidence to talk to my family about Ben and, much to my surprise, they grew, ever so slowly, to accept him. Ben came to Shabbat at my uncle's. Ben came to Passover. Ben came to my Nana and Grandpa's house. The ease of integration soothed me. The fact that I could be honest with people about my love for Ben and for Judaism made me even more faithful. I found a rabbi for the first time since twelfth grade and then had the confidence to walk back into my high school to find my first mentor. This man, who I loved and feared like family, looked me in the eye and told me he always trusted me, that he was sorry that I didn't remain Orthodox, but that he knew I would live a full life as a committed Jew. I knew I had disappointed him, that we would never be intimate parts of each other's lives, and that he still loved me. It was enough.

For the last three years, I have stopped performing my faith. I don't feel like I have to play at observance or mimic indifference. In building our home, we have argued over practice, shared the peace of Shabbat and embraced each other's family in ways that are at once equal and remarkably distinct. Marriage, in many ways, has forced me to settle into my faith, to realize that Judaism is both about the large theological questions that occupied my youth and equally about the small details that organize domestic life. I am still figuring out how to set up a Jewish home, dress like a Jewish woman, and live as a Jewish wife. But I am not frustrated by my lapses of indecision or inability to create consistency. I have grown to love unceasing new beginnings, to feel uniquely engaged as a veteran beginner at Jewish life.

Tamara Mann, 31, received her M.T.S. at Harvard Divinity School and is currently a Ph.D. candidate in American History at Columbia University. Her research interests include the history of old age, philanthropy, and charity in America. Her writing has appeared in such publications as The Washington Post, Museum, Edible Columbus *and* My Jewish Learning. *Originally from New York City, Tamara currently lives in Columbus, Ohio, with her husband and daughter.*

34 IS THE NEW "TWEEN"

By Caren Friedman

WHAT, IS HE LIKE 12 OR SOMETHING? IT FEELS LIKE decades—not just four short years—since I was the one on the bimah in place of this fresh-faced boy, speaking to the congregation about how influential the synagogue's young adult program was in my life; how as a transplant from Omaha, Nebraska, I had found a new community here in Chicago.

Where is my community now? I wonder, sitting on the cold folding chair near the back, my borrowed High Holiday ticket tucked neatly in my purse. I am grateful for my childhood friend next to me, whose presence is a comfort in a synagogue where the rabbis don't know me and the familiar faces have become few. When she heads out early with her husband and tots, I make my way to the restroom and pass moms my age hugging and wishing one another shanah tovah as they head to pick up their kids from the children's program. As I step past these happy, huggy families, I feel like a foreigner walking through their community.

Contrary to popular belief, there really are Jews in Omaha. And growing up there, I found it very easy to become involved Jewishly. From active involvement in my synagogue, a passionate love for BBYO, and beloved summers at Camp Ramah, to Hebrew High School, JCC theater, and participation in The March of the Living, it was fun and simple for me to surround myself with close Jewish friends and meaningful programs year-round. Effortless, too, was my decision to attend a university with a strong Jewish campus life, and I didn't think twice about spending a semester abroad in Israel.

Nearly 10 years ago, after graduate school (and a particularly agonizing decision-making process), I moved to Chicago, where the expanded opportunities for Jewish life eventually trumped accepting a dream-job offer in St. Louis. And easily enough, I promptly jumped into the "scene" and explored what this fabulous city of young, dynamic Jews had to offer. JUF/YLD, JCUA, YAD—I was game for the entire alphabet soup. Toss in teaching Sunday School and programs such as Makor, and I managed to build a busy Jewish life.

Several years after moving here, I made a career shift into Jewish non-profits. Suddenly, I had adoptive Jewish mothers eager to set me up, rabbi friends inviting me over for Shabbat dinners, Purim parties to attend, and enough kosher treats in the kitchen to warrant an extra weekly workout. All of these additions to my life were extraordinarily positive, and I was (and am) appreciative for all of the experiences, support, and education during that time in my life. And admittedly, a little bit of me felt like I was going to burst.

Jewish colleagues. Jewish work. Jewish lay committees. Jewish friends. Jewish social events. Jewish sports league. Jewish (obvs.) synagogue. Jewish volunteer projects.

Oh, I'd found my Jewish community all right. But balance? I wasn't feeling it. I reached a point where I needed to take a step back from my frenzied Jewish activity, breathe, and reassess. Which of these commitments were most meaningful to me? What could I add to my life to help achieve balance? How could I make the most positive contribution to the community?

Around the same time, my closest Chicago friends, in quick succession, began moving out to the suburbs, and sadder yet, back to their home-towns on the East Coast. Leaving me, at 30 years old, without the close circle of friends in the city it had taken years to build. (No one warns you that in a city full of young transplants, your friends. will. move.) Sure, I included 200 of my nearest and dearest (mostly Jewish) friends at my 30th birthday bash, but that hoopla coincided with the beginning of the end of my hyperactivity on the Jewish scene.

Perfectly timed, I was also recently single, and suddenly thrust back into the dating world—one I had thought I'd exited for the last time. I certainly wasn't thrilled about reactivating the JDate cycle, which often looked something like this:

Excited! Boys to meet! Lots of dates!
Well, that one guy was sort of cute if you dim the lights.
Annoying! Rude! Disrespectful! (And his shoes!)
Seriously? This guy is still on here? I'm so depressed.
This sucks. I need a break.
Repeat.

And off-line, all these years later, the singles scene felt even less comfortable to me than it had in my 20s. I felt ancient, over-tired, and underdressed.

Where to turn? My few single friends were younger and actually enjoyed said singles events, and my married friends were busy raising their kids in another country (you know, Northbrook), and spending nights out with other married couples. I sought out varied outlets, from book clubs to running groups, looking to build connections and a fulfilling balance. It was at this time that I did find a nice fit with the young adult community at my synagogue, eventually being chosen to represent the group and speak from the bimah about the benefits of participation. Yet, like with JDate and the Matzoh Ball, my engagement in this community was cyclical. Eventually, I felt my energy waning and began asking myself what benefits I truly was experiencing. I was slowly beginning to acknowledge and address an internal "living Jewishly" struggle that had been percolating for some time.

Not surprisingly, others in the community were at varying stages of their own journeys—several of whom I had come to enjoy spending Shabbat halted their synagogue attendance; new faces appeared and took over leadership. Walking into services and not seeing one familiar face was disconcerting. Add to that my own personal soul-searching, and my connection to the community started to waver. If I had been slow to accept this along the way, it had become infinitely clearer: engaging in the Jewish community—and any community for that matter—was much harder now than it was in my 20s.

When I began dating my current boyfriend some months later, the social environment was no less distressing. Some single friends assumed I was spending every second with him and all but dismissed me from their social calendars. Others may not have assumed that I was perpetually busy, but weren't willing to give up a coveted weekend time slot for (gasp!) someone in a relationship. And yet, we, with our new availability in happy coupledom, still didn't register with most married folks. Not quite single. Not at all married. In my 30s, I'd finally reached my tween years.

Same situation on the Jewish front. My mailbox overflowed with invitations for young Jewish singles events, young family events, and even an announcement about a new group for recently-engaged couples. The last one is a great addition to the roster, indeed. But what about those of us who don't neatly fit into those categories?

In a long-term relationship with a wonderful man whose age just misses the cut-off for "young adult" communities, we're not the target demographic for the singles scene, and we certainly wouldn't fit in at young families events, unless we borrowed our (adorable!) nieces and nephews for a day. But not engaged, we are even excluded from a group that presumably is meant to attract the rest of us. With the myriad ways to make up a family these days, it is an unfortunate reality to feel such a divide between single/married and where I fall, somewhere in between.

And so I continue to feel out options (with many yet to be explored), the cyclical excitement followed by the seemingly inevitable withdrawal—seeking the right fit for the longer-term. I continue to try to dig deeper within myself to figure out how I want to live Jewishly. Because though I sometimes move away from it temporarily, I do miss that part of my life. I feel conflicted when, on my way out to dinner, I drive by groups of men in yarmulkes walking to shul. I struggle with the fact that I didn't even renew my synagogue membership this year. I wrestle with the reality that my partner and I have vastly different takes on the topic.

I assure you that I am not waiting for the terribly specific "34-YEAR-OLD WOMEN DATING OLDER MEN CLUB" to materialize, nor do I assume joining any such club would resolve my struggle. And I'm certainly not begrudging organizations that offer quality programs to families and singles—I clearly value and have utilized them. I appreciate that as we get older, the easy ways by which we connected years ago no longer apply. Now in our 30s, my peers and I no longer live the shared experience of being poor, recent college grads living in studio apartments and exploring a new, fun city on a dime. Instead, as some create and expand their families, focus on careers and buying homes—our incomes and lifestyles becoming increasingly divergent—it is indeed hard to find relatable new friends. My mom-friends say that it gets easier with a baby, as you can bond with other mothers through playgroups/JCC/My Gym/Tot Shabbat. As a self-proclaimed tween, however, my Tot Shabbat alternative is less obvious.

Thankfully, about three years ago, I was fortunate enough to be invited to join a group of girls for dinner at a friend's apartment. In her living room, amongst veggies and six varieties of hummus, sat what appeared to be a random assortment of women. My friend, our hostess, is married with two young children. A few others also had husbands and babies at home. Another woman had just recently met a nice Jewish boy. Some were in varying stages of relationships and still others were single. My friend brought this potpourri of women together to create a monthly "Girls Night." The common thread among us: seeking connection. Unsure of how I'd fit in with this group at the outset, I talked myself into returning the next month, and then the next. Prioritizing one evening every month when JDates, boyfriends, husbands, and kids are left behind for a few hours, we come together to eat, catch up, laugh, eat, and grab a moment of calm (did I mention eat?). Three years later, the hummus and veggies have morphed into quinoa salads, apple oatmeal crisps, and chicken samosas, just as our initial loose associations have grown into sincere, comfortable friendships. (No, I'm not actually comparing my new friends to Asian pastries. But if I were, would that be so wrong?)

Since we first met, we have celebrated the woman's marriage to that nice Jewish boy. Another has become engaged. Babies have been born. Breakups have been endured and we've lost and changed jobs. We have created our own community, and in doing so, defied the stereotype that married, single and tween women can't relate. In fact, with this group, the mix is refreshing.

From the time I was young, I listened to the mahj tiles clanking, the coffee maker brewing, and my mom's merry band of mahjong mavens chattering away in the kitchen. Though I don't know a dragon from a dot or a wind, and cannot wrap my head around the complexities of building a wall of tiles, I do understand that this game was the backdrop for the network of Jewish women my mother relies on to this day. No matter that my mother is the oldest of the bunch, and was attending bat mitzvah parties for her friends' kids while they were throwing a bridal shower for one of hers. No doubt her friends had bigger houses than we did and took fancier (i.e., any) vacations. But none of that mattered in times of crisis. As their own mothers, fathers, and spouses began to fall ill and pass away, these ladies cooked, cleaned, shopped and cared for each other. At different stages in their own lives, they managed to befriend and lean on one another in spite—or because—of these differences.

The strength of our "Girls Night" community was reminiscent of my mom's circle when tragedy struck within our relatively young group. It was our reaction to the heartbreaking news—responses we undeniably learned from our Jewish mothers—which made me appreciate that I had found a Jewish connection where I had simply been looking for a connection. I realize that "Girls Night" is not an official congregation or dues-collecting organization. And I am confident that I will eventually find those types of outlets again. But in the meantime, as I continue my cultural and spiritual exploration, this little pocket of Jewish women is very welcome indeed.

Caren Friedman is approaching her 11 year Chicago anniversary, which makes her feel quite cosmopolitan when visiting Omaha. A Licensed Clinical Social Worker, she is currently putting her very expensive master's degree to excellent use directing the annual giving program at Lincoln Park Zoo. After years of feeling shunned while brunching, at 34, she has finally learned to love lox.

A FAITHFUL DECISION

By Sarah Malakoff

MY DECISION TO LIVE A JEWISH LIFE HAS BEEN A LONG time coming.

Dad, a Jewish man born and raised in inner-city Chicago, met Mom, a Catholic woman born and raised in suburban Wisconsin. And that was that.

My father fell so in love with my mother that he risked everything he knew to be with her. None of Dad's family came to my parents' wedding. And it wasn't until I came along a few years later that they started to warm up to Mom.

It's not that they didn't like her, it's that they didn't like that she wasn't Jewish. Dad was respectful of my mother's background, just as she was respectful of his. He never asked her to convert, and shortly after I was born I was baptized.

This probably isn't a unique story, but it is one that I've both embraced and struggled with for 25 years.

Jewish culture was always around me. The menorah on the mantelpiece. The shofar on the desk. The latkes for Chanukah. The trips to temple with Grandma and Grandpa. I was always aware of my Jewish heritage, and proud of it.

My teachers at church probably hated me. I asked a lot of questions. And those questions were met with answers that didn't satisfy my curiosity. Answers like "Because that's what we believe" and "The Bible says so" frustrated and perplexed me. When it came time for my Confirmation, I told my mother I didn't feel comfortable declaring I believed things that I didn't. But Mom is a rule follower and, evidently, so am I, because I did what I was told.

Scanning the course selections in college, I zeroed in on a class simply titled "Judaism." I was so eager to learn more about the religion that I identified with but didn't fully understand. The first day of class, the professor walked in, disheveled, with unkempt hair and a shoe untied. But when this local rabbi opened his mouth, the most polished, beautiful thoughts unfurled. "To know God is to be God" he would say. I felt like standing on my desk and shouting: "Finally! These are the answers to so many of my questions!"

Although I felt sure that Judaism matched my faith, morals and values, it was several years before I attended synagogue regularly and began to lead a Jewish life. Declaring that the religion I was raised in was not the religion for me was not something I took lightly. I needed that time to test myself, to question what I think is true, what I feel is important, how I want to live.

There isn't a glimmer of doubt in my decision to convert to Judaism. And, thankfully, my family couldn't be more supportive. Mom has been as respectful of my beliefs as she has always been of my father's.

As a Jew, I know that my questions might not always have answers, but that my questions are encouraged.

I know that there's something bigger out there that's too complex to understand or label.

I know that I can take guidance from and revere Torah.

I know that I will always do mitzvot because doing good is the good thing to do.

I know that I want to celebrate Shabbat and say ha-motzi with my future children.

I know that living a Jewish life is who I am and what I have always been seeking.

Even my work life is tied to Judaism, as an employee at Jewish Family and Children's Service of Minneapolis, where I'm surrounded by amazing Jewish role models every day.

It's funny how things come full circle. I, a woman brought up Catholic and raised in the Midwest, met a Jewish man born and raised on the East Coast. I couldn't have found a more perfect person with whom to share my life. Ben is my beshert. When we married each other on Nov. 6, 2010, I entered the chuppah as a woman who earnestly contemplated her beliefs for a long time, finally arriving as a Jew at the beginning of a new chapter in life.

Sarah Malakoff, 25, is the public relations/marketing communications specialist for Jewish Family and Children's Service of Minneapolis. She plays violin and would love to become proficient in Klezmer.

FOOD FIGHTS

By Becca Tanen

"WE DON'T NEED THAT!"

My Zaidie glared at my mother and put yet another container of cookies back in the cardboard box whence it came.

My Bubbie and Zaidie continued their ritual with a multitude of different food products—salad dressings loaded with fat and sugar, packages of crackers, and other highly processed foods that had no chance of finding a home in our health-conscious pantry.

Whenever my grandparents come to Maryland to pay us a visit, we are graced with loads of food we never asked for. For the next several months, we will embark on archaeological expeditions to unearth the foreign contents of our freezer. A surefire way of telling whether my grandparents have come to visit recently is by taking a quick survey of the freezer's contents:

Is every available space in the freezer filled?

Are there new items in the freezer that have so many layers of aluminum foil and plastic that it is impossible to tell what these items are?

If you answered yes to either or both of these questions, Bubbie and Zaidie have come to visit.

Jews and food have always been closely intertwined. The words *Jewish* and *deli* are practically synonymous, and we sanctify almost every ritual and holiday with food and wine. The singular ability of food to bring people together is present in every culture, and this phenomenon characterizes my upbringing. My family and I love food, but we also care about what we put into our bodies.

My family strictly follows the Jewish dietary laws of kashrut. Our kitchen at home has separate utensils, sinks and dishwashers for meat, dairy and Passover. We only eat animals that are kosher, and we do not mix dairy and meat. Everything we eat has been carefully inspected and certified before it enters our homes or our mouths.

Despite these standards, I never really felt limited by keeping kosher. My family never went hungry; on the contrary, we enjoy food with an almost illicit pleasure, a pleasure that is enhanced by the knowledge that our food choices nourish both our bodies and our souls. When we eat we serve not only ourselves, but also God.

As we advanced through the new millennium, however, my family's food choices went beyond the dietary restrictions of our ancestors and entered the realm of healthful eating. My friends have always looked at me in shock when I explain that we have never kept junk food in the house. When we were younger, my sister and I would embark on futile, yet dogged hunts for snacks.

"All we have are ingredients!" we would complain to my mother.

"Have a drink—you're probably thirsty, not hungry," was her constant refrain. "If you're still hungry, you can have a piece of fruit."

My grandparents, who constantly spoiled us with treats and sweets, who did not consider a meal complete until the table was audibly groaning under the weight of dishes, were equally dismayed. It is a mystery how they even came to obtain the junk food they thrust upon us—my grandfather is diabetic, and my grandmother is plagued with stomach issues. So, what compels grandparents to give us more food than we really *need*? When I look to their pasts, it is not difficult to answer this question.

My Zaidie was only 15 when he was forced to suffer a year in Auschwitz. By sheer chance, he and his father were spared while his mother and three siblings were sent to the gas chambers upon arrival. But if you ask my grandfather, this might not have been due to luck. When he was a boy, his Bubbie took him to visit a sainted rabbi who gave people blessings. The rabbi said to my Zaidie, "My child, you will have a long life, and nothing will happen to you." The image of the rabbi was always in his mind in the camps and served as "one of the big motivations for fighting to stay alive," because, as my grandfather explained, "I didn't want to make a liar of the rabbi."

Sometimes sheer toughness helped him survive. With pride in his voice, my Zaidie told me, "The bread they gave us was full of sawdust and also very small portions, but what happened was they gave us cheese which was inedible already; the German Army didn't use it. It was called kvarkle cheese, it was a yellow, very smelly cheese, and it was full of maggots. And some people couldn't eat it, even though they were starving. I picked it up and I closed my eyes and I closed my nose, and I knew it was protein, and I ate it...I ate the cheese with the maggots."

Sometimes a little ingenuity went a long way. When he was asked to do kitchen work, he would hide under giant billows of steam released from the lifted lids of cauldron and steal margarine. When he worked in the potato fields, he would put his special piece of thin rope through potato slices, making a hole through them and stringing them on it, hiding the slices under his clothing as he worked. Occasionally he would carry messages between camps within Auschwitz and be rewarded with a piece of bread.

Meanwhile, in Cardiff, England, my grandmother struggled with food rationing. Luckily, her mother was similarly creative with food. My Bubbie told me, "During the war we all had ration books...so my mom was very creative. She had ration books in different stores like in regular grocery stores, a vegetarian store and the kosher store."

Her father also used creative means to provide his family with food. For Passover, he made raisin wine for the four cups drunk at each Seder, and "scrounged" at farms for eggs to symbolize the circle of life in the ceremony. My Bubbie pitied the other members of the working-class area where they lived, subsisting on dried eggs "because they didn't know how to scrounge, didn't know how to get food together."

My grandmother soon developed her own methods of scrounging. Every time she visited the variety store asking for candy, they would tell her that they didn't have any. With the glee of a smug 10-year-old girl, my Bubbie told me, "I used to stand up on the box and look over the counter and say, 'What are you talking about? There's chocolate bars, I want those chocolate bars!'" She would then hide them in her closet and ration them out to her brothers with a knife.

My grandparents, like so many others who found refuge in North America, yearned to give their children and their children's children the comforts and security that they did not always have. In addition to all the food they bring us, my grandparents are constantly having friends over for meals, and every cupboard is packed with snacks. My Bubbie is happiest darting in and out of the kitchen, constantly preparing and serving more and more dishes, to such an extent that my mother practically needs to yell at her to sit down and eat. I asked my Bubbie whether growing up with food rationing contributed to her love of feeding people later in life.

"I think so," she told me, her lilting Welsh accent touched with surprise, as if she had never thought about it that way before.

"I think it's also part of my personality, because I always like to feed everybody and I'm always worried about everybody, so I always want to make sure everyone has what they like and everyone has enough of everything. And I guess it must be part of that, you know? I want to make sure no one's going hungry, no matter what their taste is, so I guess that must be part of the reason."

I have witnessed this same concern with my friends from Jewish day school and their parents, several of whom are immigrants as well. On Saturday afternoons, my friends and I float between each other's houses, all of which are within walking distance since we are forbidden to drive on the Sabbath. We immediately gravitate towards the kitchen, settle in, and peter away the last hours of Sabbath by eating and talking. Many of these Saturday afternoons in high school were spent in the kitchen at my best friend Hannah's house as we feasted on her mother's delicious Persian rice with meatballs.

Hannah's mother, Nahid, suffered horrible conditions growing up as a Jew in Iran during the Revolution. She was forced to go to Muslim school, and one day she went to a non-Jewish schoolmate's house to study. Nahid's mother had made pastries for her to bring to the schoolmate's house, but the girl's mother threw the pastries into the trash right in front of Nahid. It was their belief that Jews were impure, and so was anything they touched. Here in America, Nahid is free to cook the dishes of her homeland, and teach us their names in her native tongue.

My high school friend Eli is also a first-generation child of Jewish Persian immigrants. My friends and I would sometimes spend Sabbath afternoons at their house, where his parents barely stopped short of forcing food down our throats.

"Eat, eat!" they insisted.

"Did you get cholent?" Mr. Shamouilian inquired.

"Oh, no thank you, I'm fine with just rice," I replied nervously.

He insisted.

"I-I actually don't eat meat," I stammered.

I did not want to have to say it. I was afraid to raise my voice enough for him to hear it. As I spoke those words—as I denied the food he was offering me—I felt terrible for refusing what he, and Nahid, and my grandparents wanted so badly to give me. But a stomach condition had forced me to give up most animal products.

When I read Jonathan Safran Foer's newest book, a memoir called *Eating Animals*, I was surprised to find many similarities between it and the stories I have just related. His grandmother was also a Holocaust survivor who ate unspeakable things—but never pork—to survive. Every time she visited her grandsons, she lifted them up from under their armpits. It was not until much later that Foer realized this was not just an act of affection—she wanted to see how much they weighed. In this early portion of the book, Foer is torn between upholding his grandmother's philosophy on food and observing the vegetarianism he so strongly identifies with. While I am not a vegetarian by choice, I can easily relate to this struggle.

But the truth is, whatever I choose to eat—whether it is kosher meat or organic tofu—I will savor and enjoy every last bite of it, and never take it for granted. With each generation, my family has changed what they eat, but we will never change how we eat: with zest, enjoying every last bite until none remains. My Zaidie never gave up on the fantasy of eating more than he needed to survive, even while in the camps. He often recalls, "My biggest dream was always to be able to hold bread in one hand and a whole piece of margarine in the other and take a bite of each—that was the dream."

> *Becca Tanen, 20, is from Potomac, Maryland. She is currently an undergraduate student at the University of Pittsburgh, where she is majoring in Nonfiction Writing and Legal Studies. This past year she served as the president of the Hillel Jewish University Center at Pitt.*

TO BE A JEW IN THE WORLD

By Stacey Ballis

I JOKE AROUND ABOUT BEING JEW-ISH, THINK THAT bacon should be its own food group, and openly admit that not only have I never been to Israel, it falls way down on my list of places I want to visit, after Morocco, Spain, Ireland and China, past Portugal and South Africa, even beyond places I want to go to for a second time like Italy. I'm reasonably certain I'll get there, and I even genuinely believe I'll be moved and transformed by the experience, it's just, well, I sort of want to see Prague first.

But despite my cheek on the general subject of my Judaism, I specifically wanted to share my thoughts on Passover.

Passover has always been my favorite of the holidays. And not just because I got schickered on Manischiewitz wine when I was four. On first blush, you'd assume that it is because of the combination of food and ritual. I'm a sucker for food and ritual. When I was little, my two favorite meals to eat out were Geja's Fondue and Ron of Japan Japanese steakhouse. Whether it was cooking my own meal in tiny cauldrons on long forks to the soundtrack of classical guitar in a basement grotto, or watching quick and skilled knife work as shrimp tails flew through the air, there was something utterly delightful about those meals. Entertainment, inclusion, the comforting progression that never alters in any meaningful sense, this was heady stuff. Seductive. So no wonder that the Seder, which isn't just about eating, or just about praying, but is about using food as part and parcel of that prayer, is so appealing to that same part of me. Frankly, all it lacks is the guy juggling the salt shaker and making the onion volcano.

When I look at my life, the path I have taken in my career, the Passover Seder is essentially the culmination of everything I am passionate about. I am an educator, and the Seder is about teaching. I spent nearly a dozen years working in professional theater, and the Seder has wonderful theatrical moments, especially the "will he or won't he" ta-da moment of opening the door for the possible entrance of Elijah. I'm a writer and storyteller, and the entire service is about telling an amazing story. I'm devoted to family and friends, and the Seder is about gathering those people around you. I try to live a life that embraces diversity, and there is no greater mitzvah at a Seder than the presence of Gentiles, the sharing of our culture. And, yes, I'm a foodie who loves to entertain, so any excuse to get into the kitchen and create a great meal is a pleasure and a privilege.

My dad is on the board of Jewish Child and Family Services, a branch of Federation in Chicago, and a couple of years ago they went through a strategic planning process, during which they attempted to identify a set of core Jewish values which would help drive the work of the agency, and the direction for the future. When he shared their findings with me, I was surprised by how moved I was by the content of what they came up with. How connected I felt to the way ancient Jewish teachings, of which I have never been a student, explore the way we ought to be in the world. I realized, as I absorbed the document he sent me, that ultimately what they chose to identify as core Jewish values, are simply a set of values that should be at the core of any person. That what they describe, while beautifully supported by Jewish writings and history, are the basic values I hold dear, the ideals that I hope are infused in the way I live my life, and are values that would find equal support in the writings and teachings of other religions and cultures. That in their specificity, we find universality. That in looking into what it means to be a Jew, we find what it means to be human, and instead of underlining our differentness, we illuminate our parity.

One of the things I have always loved about the Seder, what I love in fact generally about being Jewish, is the room to grow and expand and include. I have heard that in the mid-1980s, at a conference, the topic of women rabbis was brought before a panel, and an elderly male rabbi announced to the assembly that a woman had as much place on the bimah as an orange has on the Seder plate. From that moment on, my family, like thousands around the world, have put an orange on our Seder plate, and have incorporated the story into our explanation of the sacred items it holds. We have added Miriam's Cup, a glass cup filled with water, to remind us of the second side to the story we tell.

Sometimes, as a writer, you have to go seek the story; you have to go looking for the words. Sometimes, if you are lucky, the material comes to you when you least expect it. If you had told me a few years ago that I would ever write something specifically for inclusion in any religious ritual, I'd have thought you were nuts. This is ME, after all. But I know when inspiration strikes, you have to go with it. When I read the Core Jewish Values piece my dad sent me, it immediately called to me to be part of the Seder. By the time I read it through the second time, I was already shaping it in my mind. And within a half an hour I sent it to my family, asking for their thoughts, and if they would feel comfortable incorporating it into our Seder. We did, and I was amazed once again at how seamlessly something so new fit in with something so ancient. I shared it with a few friends, who reported that they too had used it in their services with positive response.

I want to share with you the piece which is now a part of my celebration. I hope that if it resonates with you, in part or in whole, that you will feel free to use it however you like. That if you find value in it, you will send it to your friends and family. I hope that it may inspire you to create something for your own Seder, to continue to mold and shape your celebrations so that they are an accurate depiction of your own personal Jewishness. Or Jew-ishness. It is enormously gratifying to feel that no matter how secular I may choose to be, however far I get from traditional religiosity, there is room for the way I choose to practice, and I always feel genuinely embraced by my own culture.

Jewish Core Values for the Passover Seder

READER: Care for our fellow human beings is a fundamental of the Torah's outline for human life. One of the first key teachings of the Torah is that humankind was created by God in the "Tzelem Elokim"—the Divine Image. This means that all humans are worthy of respect and love. The rabbis in the Midrash teach us that only one human being was originally created. This reminds us that each one of us is equal, precious and beloved in the eyes of the Holy One. It is because of this idea that the Talmud tells us, "One who has saved a life, it is as if he has saved an entire world." Rabbi Akiva in the Talmud suggested that the verse, "V'ahavta l'reacha kamocha"—"Love your neighbor as you would love yourself" is a fundamental rule of the Torah. Thus, we are bidden to treat everyone we encounter with respect and dignity.

ALL: I will seek to respect others, and to earn the respect of others. I will remember that my own personal dignity is devalued if I treat others with contempt or intolerance. I will remember that all people are deserving of love and respect, even those who are different from me or hold different beliefs.

READER: The care for families in Jewish sources includes honoring one's father and mother—and training a child according to their way. This reminds us that our community has a distinct responsibility to help and honor families—parents and children. The last verse of the prophet Malachi reminds us that one of the Messianic goals of our people is to bring the hearts of parents and children together. As we gather for the holidays, we should remember to honor and celebrate these fundamental relationships, which are at the center of our lives.

ALL: I will seek to show love and respect to my family, both the family that I was born into, and the family I have created around myself through deep friendship. I will remember to tell my family members how grateful I am for their love, counsel, and company.

READER: Our values should push us to strive for the highest ethical behavior in all aspects of our lives. The Torah tells us "Tzedek Tzedek Tirdof"—"Righteousness, Righteousness shall you pursue." Besides the literal emphasis on just and righteous behavior, Rabbinic teaching in the Talmud and commentaries suggest that this refers to seeking peace as well as justice. Chasidic thought interprets this verse to read that both means and ends should be just and righteous. Our ideals should reflect Judaism's desire to create and sustain a community based on righteousness and peace.

ALL: I will seek to be a source of peace and fairness in my life, at home, and in my community. I will try and support others who are working for peace and justice in the world.

READER: A community has a sacred obligation to reach out to the vulnerable members of our society. Every time we do this personally or professionally, we are engaged in Holy Work, imitating the One Above who sets the example for us. "As God is merciful, so too should you be merciful," says the Talmud. By emphasizing kindness to others, we are not merely being charitable, we are actually imitating God. Elsewhere the Talmud gives specific examples of this: Just as God clothes the naked, visits the sick, buries the dead and comforts the bereaved, so too should we do these things. At a festive holiday table, we should actively remember that not all people in the world have the luxury of such abundance. When we are given opportunities to show kindness to those in need, we should welcome the chance to show our gratitude for all our blessings by helping others.

ALL: I will fill my life with acts of kindness, empathy, compassion, and charity. I am grateful for the blessings I have received in my life, and will embrace opportunities to share those blessings with others.

READER: The core values written about in Jewish teachings are values that members of any community should hold dear. Regardless of belief or religion, these values are an essential part of being a good citizen of the world. Just as the Passover Seder is an annual reminder to the Jewish people of where we have come from, in order that it shall inform where we are going, so too are these values a reminder of the best possible attributes of any member of the global community.

ALL: I will move forward with these values firmly embedded in my heart and mind. I will remember that my basic humanity insists upon respecting others, appreciating my family and friends, striving to be ethical, helping those who are in need, celebrating my personal blessings, and showing essential kindness whenever and wherever I can. This is my commitment to myself, to my community, and to the world.

Stacey Ballis, 40, is the author of five books, including Room for Improvement, The Spinster Sisters, *and* Good Enough To Eat. *She is a freelance writer and consultant in her hometown of Chicago, and is hard at work on her sixth book,* Bread and Butter, *for Berkley/ Penguin. She did her undergraduate work at Brandeis University, and makes a killer kugel.*

This essay was originally published on Oy!Chicago (www.oychicago.com).

WHY THE HECK I BECAME A RABBI

By Rabbi Taron Tachman

IMAGINE YOU AND I ARE SEATED TOGETHER ON AN airplane. You, a complete stranger to me, try to strike up a conversation. I, a rabbi, try to do everything I can to avoid the subject of what I do...my "calling."

Now, don't get me wrong. I am very proud to be a rabbi. I feel blessed, privileged, and honored to maintain such an important communal position. It's just that sometimes when I say "I'm a rabbi," strange things happen. Like people get all weird. There is astonishment, shock, bewilderment, anger and sometimes even excessive glee. Some people ask me "Why don't the Jews believe in Jesus?" Others rant about "how ALL RELIGION is evil." Still others, upon hearing I am a rabbi, start covering their mouths after uttering a swear word. (I #$% hate that!)

The list of crazy possibilities of what might happen when I say "rabbi" is truly endless. And while these and other conversations may be interesting to my seatmate, when I'm stuck in a flying metal can for three hours, such discussions do not always make for an enjoyable flight.

On the other hand, there have been many other times when blurting out to a stranger "I'm a rabbi" has led to meaningful, interesting, and heartfelt conversations. Like the time someone told me about how, as a radiologist he self-diagnosed a life threatening situation which would have certainly killed him within the hour had he not had access to the equipment and tests that indicated that he needed immediate emergency surgery. (That story still gives me chills!) Sometimes saying "I'm a rabbi" enables me to help a random person cope with a challenging life situation and sometimes I can help others see Judaism (or their own religion) in a more positive light. In such situations, an otherwise seemingly "chance" meeting seems "beshert," and it is me who learns something valuable from the encounter.

Often the question is asked of me: "Why did you want to become a rabbi?" While this question is usually asked out of sincere interest and from a place of kindness, there are occasions when I wonder if what is really being asked is: "Why THE HECK did you want to become a rabbi?" Or to put it another way: "Why would *anyone* want to do something like that?" Because to my inquisitor, the notion of dedicating one's life to God, Torah, and the Jewish people seems so ridiculous, so unfathomable, that no one in their right mind would make such a commitment.

In moments like these, when seated on an airplane next to someone who carries this approach, I have been known to avoid answering the question by creating a diversion: "HEY, LOOK THERE IS A MAN ON THE WING!!" Luckily, you, my dear airplane seatmate, are not a person with such an attitude. And since you have read this far, you no longer are a stranger. So for you, I will tell my tale.

I became a rabbi in part as a response to growing up in Grand Rapids, Michigan as one of the only Jewish kids in my public school. For me, a profoundly influential religious moment occurred when, in the midst of a holiday art project, my 3rd grade teacher announced the following: "Today we are now going to make Christmas wreaths. Everyone here is Christian, correct?" (This, in my PUBLIC school!) Upon hearing the teacher's question, my fellow students, my dear friends, all turned their gazes upon me as I sat in the center of the room, trying not to be noticed. And then, with their pointer fingers extended toward me, they excitedly exclaimed: "He's not Christian! He's a Chanukah!!"

Let's just say that I was not pleased. After all, it had only been three days (THREE DAYS) since my mom had come into the class, told my friends the story of Chanukah, fattened them up with latkes and donuts, and basically bribed them to be nice to me with delicious chocolate gelt. Sure, letting my mom "out" me as a Jew was my choice, and I don't think my friends meant me any harm. And yet, truth be told, the experience left me feeling like the loneliest Jew on the planet.

As time passed, thanks to my parents' positive Jewish modeling and some good heart-to-heart talks, I eventually embraced and took pride in my Jewish identity. No longer did questions like: "Do you guys celebrate Thanksgiving?" or "Are you guys all rich?" or "Do Jews eat carrots?" make me bristle. Instead I started to enjoy answering such questions. Soon I began to see myself as an "ambassador to Judaism." Being an ambassador meant that what I said and what I did really mattered. It also meant that I needed to know as much as I could about that which I was representing. No, I didn't score any converts, (I didn't try) but I didn't get beat up either.

As good as this "ambassador" role was, I found myself often longing to be among others who understood me. I pined for people who knew the secret Jewish handshake, people who also had "Dayeinu" stuck in their heads, and people who, like me, knew the truth about Santa. In time, I found my "peeps" at Jewish summer camp, youth group, synagogue and in college. In a sense, it was this search for my people that led me to the Rabbinate. And what I found while searching for Goldsteins, Schwartzs and Cohens was a profound love of God, Torah, Jewish texts, rituals, music, ethics and values, Israel and more. At the same time, I realized that Judaism has something important to say about how we lead our lives.

By the way, the decision to become a rabbi didn't come easily. I agonized for a long time, wondering if I was right for the job or if it was right for me. It seemed to me that I had the right personality to succeed, I just wasn't so sure about God. After much soul searching, praying, and writing, I finally decided to apply to rabbinical school and though I still have lots of questions, (thank God) I know I made the right choice.

There's so much I love about being a rabbi: I love people and being a rabbi means getting paid to be a mensch. I love having the chance to encourage, teach, and to inspire others to do good in the world—like working at Temple Sholom's weekly soup kitchen, or building a house in New Orleans to help flood victims. I love sharing with others Jewish texts which teach us to be more moral, holy and ethical people and help us to improve our relationships. Being a rabbi also means having the honored privilege to be invited into people's lives during some of their most joyous moments—like standing under the chuppah with a couple while officiating a wedding—(How cool is that?) and it means extending a hand of support to a family in their darkest moments when the ground suddenly crumbles beneath their feet.

Quick story—recently in the midst of a happy celebration of my birthday in Michigan I received a heartbreaking phone call informing me of the tragic death of a young person. It was clear that I needed to return home immediately to comfort the family. As you can imagine, this call was the last thing I wanted to receive on my birthday. And yet, as strange as it may sound, this phone call, received on my birthday, served for me as a ringing reminder of why I was born, and what God has called me to do on this earth. (I hope I am doing a good job!)

Admittedly, I don't always succeed, and sometimes I find myself awake at night thinking about what more could be done. What keeps me going is the sustaining comfort of our loving and caring God and my faith in the power of Jewish tradition and community. My own losses too have made me even more aware of how God, community and tradition can be a source of comfort in times of need. For example, I had only been at Temple Sholom a month when my own younger brother and only sibling died suddenly. I will never forget the kindness and caring of the Temple Sholom community who at this time barely knew me. To be a part of this Temple during those trying times felt to me and my family as though angels had descended upon our broken-hearted home and had enclosed us in the loving shelter of their wings.

Listen—I could go on and on about what I love about my "calling." Were there more time, I might talk about having a relationship with God or how praying, studying and being an active part of a Jewish community can make such a positive difference in one's life. I'm sure there are a hundred other topics I could discuss as well, but alas, I think the plane is landing soon.

Ordained in 2004 by the Hebrew Union College-Jewish Institute of Religion in New York, Rabbi Taron Tachman, 40, earned his undergraduate degree in Psychology at Michigan State University. He went on to earn a Master's of Social Work at the University of Michigan and a Certificate in Jewish Communal Service and Judaic Studies from the Sol Drachler Program in Jewish Communal Leadership at the University of Michigan. Following his Graduate Studies at Michigan, Rabbi Tachman served as the Campus Hillel Director at Eastern Michigan University where he helped establish a new and vibrant Hillel Center. Rabbi Tachman has also received national recognition for his efforts to attract and engage Young Adults in their 20's and 30's to Temple Sholom. In addition to his work at the Temple, Rabbi Tachman serves on the Associates Division Executive Committee of the Jewish Council on Urban Affairs, is a rabbinic liaison to the Sidney N. Shure Kehilla Program and is a regular contributing blogger to Oy!Chicago, a blog reaching upwards of 30,000 people a year.

This essay was originally published on Oy!Chicago (www.oychicago.com).

VOLITION

By Tera "Nova Jade Greene*

I'D LIKE TO THINK OF MYSELF AS A GREAT VOLUNTEER. Volunteering is one of my many wonderful gifts. It is how I have helped, and will continue to help, repair the world. In fact, I believe volunteering is how I came into being a human on this planet in the first place. Being Jewish means caring for the whole of society, not just ourselves; but being me, I express myself with caring for others because I am an Outsider's Outsider, made from the fabric of Minorities.

Of my own volition, and in no particular order (and without going into further subsets of my major identities): I am proudly Black, gratefully Jewish, beautifully Woman and joyfully Homosexual. I believe that when I was a tiny Soul in Hashem's Factory, just before finding myself incubating in the warmth of my mother's womb, G-d said to all of us Being Made, "A volunteer is needed right away to be the epitome of an Outsider. But, do not worry. Whomever volunteers will not only have My Guidance every step of the way, but you, Soul, will also arrive at the uttermost feeling of Peace."

The Hand of My Soul created a great wind, and I awoke in this body, memory erased of What Had Just Happened, but poised to find my way. . .

My particular sense of Self has been shaped by my peculiar sense of identification with "The Others." Although my own Otherness and my ability to relate to

"The Other" is what defines me, making me whole and allowing me to live a passionate and sincere life, I have struggled into the ownership of my existence as easily as I have questioned my own Identity, and parts therein. When I volunteered way back before my time in Hashem's Factory, I suppose I did not know what I was getting myself into, but That Guidance I was promised has always been felt. Through every "wrong" turn, through every serendipitous occasion, I have come to choose and embrace my Race, my Religion, my Gender (though it is fluid, non-conforming), and my Sexuality. Symbiotically, these major pieces of my Self have also chosen and embraced me.

My Identity. It wraps me up like a Tallit, binding me to G-d and to my True Self.

My Identity is a beautiful, colorful puzzle, bursting with talent and comprised of the Underdog.

In infant and adolescent years I was raised by a single-parent father. Thereafter, I was parented by my paternal grandfather. Yes, I was born female, but in this medically scientific age of transformation, I very well could have decided against embracing the Underdog of Womanhood that was placed before me. But, after much wrestling with teaching myself how to have a happy menstrual cycle and learning how to balance my masculine energies with my female energies, among other things, I knew I was hooked. I choose to be my own kind of Woman, and how I portray my Womanhood fits me just right. The Woman that I have put together is humorous, strong, sensitive, intelligent and unapologetically real.

How does one "choose their race"? The same way they choose *not* to relate to their race. Not until I hit my 20s did I start to really identify as Black. In my early years, I lived in places where my family of two was the only Black family around. I skipped two grades and through high school, rarely did I have many People Who Looked Like Me in my honors or AP classes. Not that I was actively choosing not to relate to my racial background (to which I note is also a paint bucket that includes Irish and Native American blood), but I just did not have a lot to go on in the way of knowing *how* to relate to Them, and subsequently, to Myself. But, I got older, and I chose to embrace my heritage more happily as I learned about our great contributions in history, like peanut butter, the traffic light and jazz and rock 'n roll. I learned just how lovely my people are and more so, how I can help to lift my people up as I learn to understand our struggles and find solutions to ameliorate our community's situation.

I choose to be Black, with reddish-golden undertones in my skin and hair that is fun-to-boot because there's so much hope in our sinews.

Choosing to declare outwardly to my father that I was attracted to the same sex when I was 12 years old was not easy, but it was a lot more easily done because the outcome was positive after I expressed the Honest Truth bestowed upon me by G-d. Choosing to be a visible lesbian in my professional work is a blessing—not for me, but for all those in the world who are oppressed and cannot be out in their lives. When I volunteer at LGBTQ film festivals, march in parades or rallies for equality . . . when I blog with the first ever gay blog at the *Jewish Journal Online* or when I hear my first comedic short is screening at the UNAIDS Joint United Nations Conference in Mumbai or in a small Midwestern town, I place one more drop in the sea that raises awareness and equality for all people. I choose to be my truthful sexual identity because it gives me a platform to speak my voice and stand in my Courage to Be, which in turn, paves the way for more people to do the same.

Being Jewish is about action. How you approach your Jewishness, and how you create a world that is livable for yourself, the people of the world, and the people of the world yet to come is the beauty of the Action(s). Being Jewish is about caring for the "Other," the stranger . . . Being Jewish, to me, is especially about volunteering yourself to do the right thing, to express your Truths, and to question, probe and innovate.

Being Jewish and how I express my Jew-Self, is just as unique to me as it is uniquely you. That is why after "shopping around" to so many religious beliefs since I first began to read a Bible when I was about eight years old, I came home to Judaism. Why? Because while I was wrestling with my Spiritual Self, G-d was guiding me through. Judaism was a gentle magnet attracted to me for decades before I had my "Ah-ha!" moment one day and decided to choose to convert.

Who I am is no easy task; historically, the pieces of my Self Puzzle on an individual level have not been easy to be either. But that is why I am here. That is why I volunteered to come to live on Earth—to be Guided by G-d and be the example that Women, Jews, Homosexuals and people of Black heritage are all Good. We may be minorities, but look at all the positive things these communities have contributed amidst countless persecution! With that kind of lineage, I have no choice but to gladly choose to express who I am with all of my energy because just by being here, I have already brought four communities together, thusly repairing the world on a microcosmic scale; and henceforth, embodying shalom—peace, completeness.

I'm not here to judge, just here to inspire, and living in my Jewishness affords me the platform to live life and do it in the way that I choose.

Tera "Nova Jade Greene, 26, resides in Los Angeles, CA. At the time of this writing she is a contributing blogger to "Oy Gay," the Jewish Journal's first ever LGBTQ Blog. A musician by trade, Nova Jade* is also a film producer, an artivist, poet and educator. She can be found at http://www.twitter.com/djnovajade, which has a link to her personal website and constant updates from her World of Happenstances.*

SURVIVING MIKVAH 101

By Rachel Friedman

I HATE WATER. I DON'T LOVE DRINKING IT, I'M NOT a swimmer—not even to cool off while sunbathing—and as my college roommates can attest, I went through a phase where the shower and I were basically frenemies, interacting only when absolutely necessary.

Thankfully, I've grown up enough to recognize that even though I hate getting wet, showering is non-optional. However, even on the hottest of summer days, you couldn't pay me to jump into the pool and I can provide a 100% guarantee that I will never step into Lake Michigan.

So when my rabbi informed me that I'd have to visit the mikvah before I got married, I panicked. For those not familiar with the mikvah, rest assured—you are not alone. I didn't know much about it myself until I found out I'd be going.

According to Orthodox Judaism, a bride must visit the mikvah before the day of her wedding, as a ritual of purification before entering the chuppah and getting married. As a not-so-Orthodox Jew, I had a lot of questions—and the mikvah lady was there to answer all of those questions and more.

The mikvah lady, otherwise known as my rabbi's mother-in-law, walked me through the process. We toured the building, which looked more like a spa than a scary bath house, and she asked me a lot of awkward questions about my sex life, my menstrual cycle, and my plans for starting a family. I asked her about the technicalities, what I would

74

need to do to prepare for my visit, and most importantly, how long I'd actually have to be underwater. And while it was mortifying talking about premarital sex and family planning with a lady my grandma's age, it was a very eye-opening discussion. As I am certainly not an expert in the Jewish laws of Mikvah, Nidah and family purity, I encourage those harboring curiosity to learn more about it. Riveting stuff.

Back to the story. After wrapping up my Mikvah 101 course, I scheduled my appointment for my pre-wedding dunk and promptly put the whole issue at the back of my mind. I returned to sorting out seating charts, confirming last-minute details with vendors, and finalizing honeymoon plans.

At last, the day was upon me. No—not my wedding day. Dunk day. I arrived at the mikvah and spent about 20 minutes preparing: shampooing and combing my hair, exfoliating my skin, and removing my nail polish. I took out my contacts, because no foreign objects are allowed into the mikvah (not even ones that keep you from stumbling into the mikvah by accident). And then I hit the buzzer to let the mikvah lady know that I was ready to head in.

It was only when I stepped into the water that the mikvah lady and I found out that the water heater was broken. Just my luck—the girl with the water aversion stuck in a freezing cold mikvah. Luckily, the only requirement is that you are completely submerged for literally one second, three times.

Quickly, I repeated after the mikvah lady as she helped me say the prayer before plunging into the pool and then, about six seconds later, it was over.

I know many brides who have described their experience at the mikvah as a deeply spiritual moment. For me, my connection to Judaism is rooted more in tradition and community than spirituality, and despite the technical difficulties, I left the mikvah feeling a profound connection to the Jewish women over dozens of generations who had gone through this ritual cleansing.

And if thousands of other women could suffer through getting wet long enough to start a marriage with a clean slate, I could too.

Rachel Friedman, 26, is from Solon, Ohio, but lives in Chicago. She is the director of Volunteers and Outreach at The ARK. As a transplant to a new city, she often cannot make it home for Jewish holidays so she tries to host holiday meals and parties: Passover Seder for friends, Chanukah parties and break fast dinners for Yom Kippur.

This essay was originally published on Oy!Chicago (www.oychicago.com).

INGESTING JUDAISM

By Jessica Kirzane

I STARTED BAKING CHALLAH AS A COLLEGE STUDENT reveling in her very first kitchen. I liked that it was complicated and new, something my mother had never done at home, something I could claim as entirely my own. I liked the feel of the dough in my hands, the weight and heft of it, its soft, sticky warmth, its sweet, comforting smell. I liked the time that it took to make the challah, the sense that it was very present in my life, not like a fleeting batch of cookie dough that is made and baked and finished, but something that must wait for hours to be tended to. I would sit next to my bowl of rising dough, doing my homework and noticing as the dough slowly rose and took its form. Most of all, I liked to be the kind of person who would bake her own challah, the kind of person who could invite her friends over and provide them with a hot loaf fresh from the oven, its lopsided braids proclaiming how very homemade it was, how very quaint and earnest and traditional.

Baking challah was a tradition of my own invention. I learned it from books and claimed it as my own, never having watched a parent, grandparent, or even older friend perform the magic of pouring yeast and water, flour and eggs, into a bowl to create a small work of art. Challah baking was something entirely new for me, part of my attempt to reinvent myself as an adult. And yet it was profoundly, and even self-consciously, an act of nostalgia, and of yearning. I was projecting myself into an imagined past, tying myself into a line of challah-baking women that I believed must be part of my family somewhere down the line. In doing so I was asserting my authenticity as the kind of Jew who would bake challah, even though I had learned it from a recipe book given to me as a birthday present by my non-Jewish best friend. I made challah in the way that my sister and I had died bandanas in tea when we were children, pretending to be characters in *Little House on the Prairie*. It was an attempt to live in a world outside of my own. I was transforming my own kitchen into a vessel of the past, refusing to use an electric mixer so that my dough would be somehow more pure, more a product of my own hands, infused with my own spirit.

As whimsical, imaginative, and almost playful as the act was, at the same time, I made challah as an act of devotion; I did it prayerfully and with a sense of wonder. The smell of my kitchen on a Friday afternoon became a kind of prayer for me; it created a sense of Shabbat that nothing else could produce in me so consistently and so profoundly. My challah baking was an exercise in role playing, but I liked it so much that I incorporated that role into my sense of self, into my engagement with the infinite and into the weekly patterns of my life.

I have been baking challah every week for about three years, and I don't believe that I will ever stop. Each week I share my bread with friends, and as they mumble words of appreciation between bites of the fresh, honeyed loaf, I feel a sense of pride so deep that I have to check it by saying to them, "It's really not that hard, you know, to make challah," or, "Last week's was better, I think." What I am really feeling is that they are ingesting a part of me, a product of my hands that asserts my very identity. Making challah has transformed how I see myself as a Jew, has moved my experience of Judaism from knowledge to physical action, and made it part of my day-to-day life in a way that no amount of books or songs was ever quite able to do. And because it is so physical, I can share it with people in a much more concrete way than teaching or recommending a book, or even praying together allows. People enter my home and they don't just experience Judaism or talk about Judaism, they eat Judaism. As imaginative as my relationship to challah is, what could be more real and basic than the act of ingestion?

Challah invites community. There is far too much for one person to eat, and so my weekly bread-baking requires a gathering of friends, eager to partake. My friends, none of whom bake challah as regularly is I do, have come to anticipate my challah—it has become a part of their Jewish lives to know that when they come to my home, they will eat my challah. And I think for them my challah is more clearly traditional than it is for me—they don't know from whom I learned to make challah, I could very well be carrying on a family recipe, rather than studying it in a recipe book. But I do know that they find the challah charming, that it feels like tradition to them, that eating it connects them to a sense of Jewishness, and that I am opening up that opportunity to them through the smells and tastes of my kitchen. Baking challah allows me to give an opportunity to my friends to experience Judaism on a sensual level, which is so important for so many of us who experience Judaism largely academically.

Perhaps my entire relationship to Judaism and Jewishness, which encompasses so much of my life, is a nostalgic and romantic exercise that has become so firmly entwined in the practicalities of my everyday life, like buying yeast and kneading dough, that it has become as concrete as it is imaginary, and it is hard to tell where the longing ends and the reality begins. I am an atheist longing to believe in God so deeply that more often than not, I truly do believe. I am an American Jew born in an English-speaking home who studies Yiddish and Hebrew with the hope of mastering them as mother tongues, even though I think, feel, and love in English. My Judaism is as real and as impossible as faith, it is in every daily detail of my life, and yet I often have occasion to wonder if Judaism is what I do, or if it is who I am. But all of these questions aside, the complicatedness of my relationship to God, tradition, language, and culture aside, Judaism is something practical and concrete that ties me to my community and nourishes me as fully as bread. Even as I may question the traditionalism, the legitimacy, the purity of my Jewish experience, it is as present and as concrete, as basic and indeed as necessary as the challah on my Shabbos table.

Jessica Kirzane, 24, is a student in Yiddish Studies at Columbia University. She grew up in New Jersey, England, and Virginia, and graduated from the University of Virginia with a degree in Jewish Studies and English Language and Literature. She is married to an HUC rabbinical student, and they currently live in NYC.

MY GRANDFATHER'S BOXES

By Dan Gordon

MY SISTER AND OUR COUSIN RECENTLY HAD THE privilege-chore of going through boxes upon boxes of our grandfather's belongings, which had resided for years in my parents' basement. The insight we gained about our family, and about life—and how it's changing—is worth sharing.

In 1997, about a month from his 89th birthday, Grandpa moved to Bloomington-Normal, Illinois, to serve as interim rabbi for Moses Montefiore Congregation. At the time Grandpa moved to my hometown, the only thought that gave me pause was that he most likely would be there at the end of his life. And so he was, a blessed eight years later.

A Reform rabbi since 1933 and a collector of things all his life, my grandfather had too many boxes to fit in his small apartment, and many of them found their way to my parents' basement when Grandpa first moved to town. My parents sorted through some of them with him, but they barely made a dent.

That gave my sister Rachel and cousin Adina their opportunity this summer. I take two conflicting lessons from what they found.

Lesson No. 1: Get rid of stuff. Among the less useful items: a tax return from 1952, airplane boarding passes from as far back as the 1960s, instruction manuals for seemingly everything he ever purchased, old hearing aids, a soup ladle.

Lesson No. 2: Keep stuff. Rachel and Adina report that in a bitter-sweet way, they know Grandpa better now than ever before. And not just Grandpa, but his parents and siblings and wives (widowed in 1983, he remarried in 1986 and was widowed a second time in 1997).

Among the treasures is a letter his father wrote his mother in 1899 arguing a point about Jewish observance. There is a copy of my great-great-grandfather's citizenship certificate from the 1890s, a detailed accounting book, coins minted in the late 1890s and very early 1900s.

From a 1915 brochure for the Minneapolis Talmud Torah religious school, which his father had founded: "If we can only save a few of the boys from the saloons, pool halls and low dance halls, and make them good men, we feel that our money is well spent."

Hand-written on a scrap of paper: "Lord grant me the senility to forget the people I never liked anyway, the good fortune to run into the ones I do like, and the eyesight to tell the difference."

Even more amazing are the letters. Grandpa was a correspondent, not in the media sense but in the keeping-in-touch-before-email sense. He kept copies of many letters he wrote and nearly everything people sent to him.

As a rabbi, he was an important presence in many people's lives. He received (and saved) scores of notes with messages such as, "I was so touched by your sermon..." and "Thank you so much for what you said at my brother's funeral..." Then there are the thank-you notes he received from (evidently) an elementary school class that had toured his congregation, Main Line Reform outside Philadelphia, in 1959. Most resemble this first (reprinted exactly as written):

> Dear Rabbi Gordon,
> I enjoyed it tremendously. Thanks for telling us the difference between Orthodox and Reformed.
> Your friend,
> Mark Lehman
> p.s. You're nice.

And oh, the love letters. The first are from the 1920s with my grandmother and continuing through their marriage; then a collection that started in the 1980s with Florence, his second wife; and then, yes, after age 90, correspondence with a woman who lived in England but with whom it seems he would have spent considerable time had she lived closer.

It is striking that our grandchildren will not have this same opportunity. Grandpa wrote letters. Today we write quick emails, use abbreviations in text messages, update our Facebook statuses. Our histories won't look the same on Yahoo!

Yet even if putting pen to paper is much rarer today than it was a generation ago (or three), some gems from the collection are timeless:

"Wishing...Enough happiness to keep you sweet, Enough trials to keep you strong, Enough sorrow to keep you human, Enough hope to keep you happy, Enough failure to keep you humble, Enough success to keep you eager, Enough friends to give you comfort, Enough wealth to meet your needs, Enough enthusiasm to look forward, Enough faith to banish depression, Enough determination to make each day better than yesterday."

Send that one to your kids—or your parents—with a handwritten note. It's too long for Twitter.

Dan Gordon is a freelance writer, editor, and social-justice advocate living in Arlington, Va. He writes a monthly column for the Washington Jewish Week *and is a member of the Hebrew Immigrant Aid Society's Young Leaders group in Washington, D.C. Dan also recently completed a leadership-training program with Jews United for Justice in Washington and is a member of Agudas Achim Congregation in Alexandria, Va. Born in Normal, Ill., he graduated magna cum laude from the University of Missouri with a bachelor's degree in journalism (news/editorial). He is an amateur musician who, when he's not contra or swing dancing, enjoys playing the violin and singing.*

This essay was originally published August 27, 2009 in the Washington Jewish Week.

HOW DO YOU DEFINE ME?

By Farrah Fidler

THERE COMES A TIME IN EVERYONE'S LIFE WHEN THEY consider online dating. "Too religious" for JDate (I keep Shabbat and kosher), but not necessarily religious enough for Frumster (I've been known to sunbathe on Shabbat), I often struggle with which box to check and which label to apply to my Judaism. Am I somewhere on the line that spans widely in Modern Orthodoxy? While applying that label loosely, it always feels like a sweater that never fit right.

Having started my religious journey nine years ago, I've had the privilege of slipping in and out of various circles that range from Chabad houses and Upper West Side "fashion show" Shabbats to Kabbalah Centres and soul searchers who are a little lost now and then. See, I know the lingo now, and I secretly get great joy out of surprising religious men who stick out like sore thumbs in Brooklyn bars with my knowledge of halacha (Jewish law) while I'm wearing clothing that isn't modest. The looks on their faces are priceless, and I see the cogs turning trying to figure out how I know the things I do and what brought me to this place. They don't come from where I do, and while their Saturday night outing is somewhat of an escape from their sheltered existence, I'm just doing what I've always done—grabbing some drinks with my girlfriends, only lately we talk about the coming of moshiach (the Messiah).

Sometimes this doesn't work in my favor. Sometimes when I see an attractive man with a covered head, lightly bearded face, rocking tzitzit, I wish I looked like a baal tshuvah stereotype. The spitting image of a girl trying to fit in and serve G-d at the same time. Because if I'm not wearing a skirt down to my knees and sleeves that cover my elbows—the Orthodox uniform—how else will he know that we practice Judaism very similarly? Well, conversation might help, and I might throw out terms that only "insiders" know, but I always feel like I'm trying too hard. That I'm too desperate to be recognized as "one of them."

It wasn't until this past Rosh Hashanah that I stopped thinking about how to classify my Jewish identity and I allowed myself to be defined. When I showed up at my friend's building, I bumped into another guest who had just arrived. Because of my outfit (long sleeves underneath an otherwise sleeveless dress), he asked if I was frum (religious). "Ish," was my answer. Later in the evening seated around the dinner table with friends, after discussing with one in particular what a Neo Chassid is, we all had a chance to go around the table and share a story or thought with our fellow diners. When it was my turn, I shared my shofar experience. I told them all about how my soul exploded when I heard the shofar blast for the first time this year. How I had a one-on-one with the Big G. Offered myself as an empty vessel to be filled with His kindness, and prayed for a joyful year. I must say, I got some interesting stares. And then . . . "Your soul exploded?! Of course you're a Neo Chassid!"

A week later I am still embracing this title. Sometimes I laugh at it and don't take it seriously. Isn't a Neo Chassid just some kid who wants to be spiritual without any religious practice? Maybe. Or maybe the new definition can be shaped by the individual. So my version of Neo Chassidism is being a girl in her 20s who wears pants when she wants to (and if she gives them up it's simply because summer is too hot for jeans), prays earnestly during soul-shattering Rosh Hashanah services, hits up the bar on Saturday night drinking and shooting the breeze about when the Messiah comes, and makes sure to observe the Fast of Gedaliah the next day, even if the religious men at the bar tell her she doesn't have to.

Farrah Fidler is a public relations and social media consultant. She is a self-proclaimed Neo Chassid who lives in Brooklyn with two fabulous roommates: one non-observant Jew and one Catholic.

Together they blog on the religion site, Busted Halo, at http://www.bustedhalo.com/category/girlsmeetg-d. Because so much of her work is immersed in the Jewish world, after a week filled with Jew-centric events she has been known to say "I need a Gentile-only vacation." Farrah was an original cast member in the storytelling/spoken-word show Birthright Israel Monologues, which toured major cities in the US.

This essay was originally published on bustedhalo.com.

THE BEST KEPT SECRET IN JEWISH MARRIAGE

By Nina Badzin

MY HUSBAND AND I WERE MARRIED FOR FIVE YEARS, together for seven, when I suggested we learn about the laws of family purity.

"The laws of *what*?" he said.

I told him that we wouldn't touch for a certain amount of days each month until I went to the mikvah. Baffled, he wondered if I might consider changing the dishes during Passover before I started worrying about "something like that."

See, I'd upset the balance of Judaism in our relationship. Bryan was "the religious" one, the one who'd been a member at a Conservative synagogue all his life, a camper and counselor at Ramah, the one who could read Torah on short notice. On Shabbat mornings he brought our son to the same synagogue where his grandfather and father had been board presidents. He was the one who encouraged me to register for two sets of dishes, the one who eagerly awaited a Shabbat feast every Friday night. Now I, the one who covertly turned on my cell phone during his and our son's Saturday afternoon nap, their "Shabbos menucha," was saying that it was hands off for 12 days each month, that he couldn't so much as pass me one of our meat *or* dairy plates.

He thought I'd lost my mind. While Bryan's background in the Conservative movement gave him a deep yearning for a Jewish home, he didn't know that laws existed guiding the physical relationship between a husband and wife.

Our wedding was the perfect example of our confusing Jewish beginning as a couple. We got married in Chicago by the same Reform rabbi who married my parents and officiated at my bat mitzvah. And although this rabbi was supportive of our plans to observe the traditions of the tish (gathering of the men around a table) and the hakanesset kallah (gathering of the women to greet the bride), he didn't suggest I visit the mikvah before the big day. The idea hadn't occurred to Bryan, either. It seemed that the only wedding rituals that Bryan and I knew about were the ones we'd witnessed first hand at the wedding of a traditional friend. Our non-Jewish wedding planner was the one who taught us about yichud (the brief seclusion of the bride and groom after the ceremony), and we included that custom, too.

Then five years later, seemingly out of nowhere, I came home with my big pronouncement about family purity without telling him the real source of my inspiration—a non-affiliated friend of mine who casually mentioned abstaining from any contact with her husband for about two weeks and then visiting the mikvah. "Are you kidding?" I'd asked her, unable to understand why this particular friend would do something "so Orthodox." It wasn't that I'd never *heard* of a mikvah, I'd just never heard of someone "like me" going. "It does wonders for your sex life," she said without blushing.

I was intrigued. Did I mention that my husband and I had been together for seven years?

Coincidentally, soon after hearing about the steamy benefits of family purity, I was invited to a fundraiser for Minneapolis' new mikvah, an event that attracted women from every denomination. All of us smiled as the speaker, an exuberant rebbetzin from Borough Park, used the metaphor of cooking to inspire the audience. The most exotic, most delicious stews, she insisted, were enjoyed only by those who let the pot simmer for . . . something like 12 days. She made a wife's evening at the mikvah at the end of the time apart from her husband sound like a luxurious, spiritual spa-like retreat. And she used plenty of other food euphemisms to give us an idea of the spicy situation that would follow at home.

I was shocked, but I seemed to be in the minority. The Orthodox women in the audience had been nodding knowingly the entire time, along with the wives of the Conservative rabbis. "I didn't realize that non-Orthodox couples do this," I said quietly to the rabbis' wives that I knew personally from our synagogue. They explained that the private nature of the laws of family purity is one of the most beautiful aspects of the mitzvah. "Nobody has to know but you and your husband." But that was the problem, I thought. *Nobody knows.*

My intrigue turned into frustration at the idea that I'd never encountered this information before. I realized quickly, however, that I wasn't being fair. After all, Bryan and I weren't married by a Conservative rabbi, and because we'd moved to Minneapolis in the middle of our engagement, we'd missed the window for the marriage classes at Beth El. Maybe the benefits of family purity weren't being treated as a secret, maybe they were only a secret to Bryan and me.

I took an informal poll of my friends around the country who were married by Conservative rabbis in the past 10 years. As it turned out, several visited the mikvah before their weddings, but they knew little about family purity. Those who knew *something* about it didn't consider it an option. "Isn't it denigrating to women?" I heard. *Who are "they" to tell us that we're not clean? Why would anyone want to be naked in front of some strange woman? Why would anyone want to take a dip in some strange pool?*

By the time I found a study partner who could help me answer these questions for myself, I was already pregnant with our second child. That afforded me plenty of time to study the laws. (A woman doesn't visit the mikvah unless she has menstruated.) I examined the *how* and the *when* and the *why* of both the days of separation between spouses and the actual evening at the mikvah. We also spent a good portion of our sessions discussing the aspects that some saw as an insult to women, looking at the text, reading commentaries on the text, and reading commentaries on the commentaries of the text. My teacher encouraged me try it and make my own choice. "If it doesn't feel right," she said, "you won't do it again. What's the harm?"

Four years later I'm something of an unofficial public relations person for our mikvah—evidence enough that participating in the tradition does not feel like a contradiction of my identity as a strong, independent Jewish woman. But I wouldn't expect anyone to take my word for it. The only way to form fair conclusions is to learn about the laws and talk to people who observe them. I hope that in time we'll see more opportunities for open conversation because if our grandmothers and mothers and friends don't observe taharah hamishpacha, or if they have preconceived notions about the practice, then how will a new generation discover the potential benefits?

The benefits, of course, run deeper than the lure of an "exotic stew." Yes, my interest in family purity *began* with my friend's promise of a magically improved connection with my husband. But I've *continued* observing the laws for other, unexpected connections such as one to God and to my heritage. Every time I submerge myself in the water of the mikvah, I perceive an intangible lifeline between the past and the future. And I sense my secure place in that line, even if I'm still addicted to my cell phone seven days a week and my Passover kitchen isn't exactly up to snuff. I'm working on those aspects of my observance, too. I just wish I could find a way to make it as much fun as adding new, spicy ingredients to an old, familiar dish.

Nina Badzin, 34, is a writer from Highland Park, IL. She now lives with her husband and their three children in Minneapolis. If she absolutely had to put a label on her Judaism, she'd call it "Reformadox." She loves the traditional aspects of Judaism, but she likes to cherry-pick them too.

*A version of this essay was first published in
CJ: Voices of Conservative/Masorti Judaism in September 2010*

UNPLUGGING EXPECTATIONS

By Donald C. Cutler

IN SEPTEMBER OF 2008, I LEFT THE WARM EMBRACE of the professional Jewish world to enter the for-profit sector. It became clear that I needed a place for the High Holidays and to call my own Jewishly, in that my work environment would no longer be Jewish in content. I needed a Jewish home to learn, celebrate, and work for the community.

I found a congregation on the Upper East Side of New York, near where I live. I am not going to lie here, the $18/year under-30 membership did help matters. So, with my wife, I joined Temple Shaaray Tefila just in time for some High Holiday action.

After the beginning of the year, I started receiving invitations to Shabbat Unplugged services, catering to the 20s and 30s set in the congregation. I began to go to these cohort-specific services to see what was happening. I was married, so I didn't need a meat market, and I have a strong Jewish identity, so I didn't need a line-by-line explanation, both real concerns with traditional outreach to this community within the Reform movement.

But I was pleasantly surprised to find a prayerful and intentional community of committed Reform Jews of my generation engaged in a local congregation. Shabbat Unplugged won't do it for everyone and I wouldn't begin to pretend it is a panacea for the involvement of younger Jews in traditional congregational life. But it is a real start.

89

These services address many of the issues that my generation often complains about regarding stuffy Reform congregations. And by way of voting with our feet, people seem to be pro-Shabbat Unplugged. When I started going to these services there were about 50 to 75 people on a good night. Now we run out of chairs, topping out at about double the early attendance numbers. The organizers like to joke that the sushi oneg is what brings people in, but really it is the desire for a real, accessible and meaningful Shabbat experience, that brings people in and keeps them coming back.

People, no matter the age, are looking for meaning. The organized Jewish community, a term many active and unengaged 20- and 30-something Jews shun because of its general lack of understanding of this age group, is the logical place for Jews to find this meaningful experience. However, when a group of people with no connection to another group of people makes choices about how to reach out and provide meaning, the other group will neither care nor find meaning. A vast majority of programming created for us adults is created by people who have not been part of our cohort for nearly a generation. Perhaps this is why Shabbat Unplugged works for our community.

Back when this all started, the "young people" got together with the "young" rabbi to discuss what they wanted. In some places that might have been more educational nights that talk about sexuality or social action events or even nothing at all. But at Shaaray Tefila, there was a desire for a different kind of service and so they created one.

Services include community song, an approachable d'var Torah-based sermon, time to kibitz and, yes, a sushi oneg. But there is a sense of community that is real here that I have not seen regularly in other places and is the number one reason I have continued as a member of this Temple after my introductory under-30 membership turned into a more traditional congregational membership (read: more money).

Donald C. Cutler is an analyst at Kekst and Company, a corporate and financial communications firm in New York City. He previously was the Communications Manager for the Union for Reform Judaism, where he helped launch RJ.org, News and Views of Reform Jews, to which he still contributes. He also writes for Jewschool.com, a progressive Jewish blog. Donald currently serves as a member of the Reform Jewish Voice of New York State Steering Committee, leading its Marriage Equality initiative and along with his wife Abby is a member of Temple Shaaray Tefila on the Upper East Side of Manhattan.

A version of this essay was originally published on Jewschool.com.

90

THE RUMORS OF HER DEATH

By Libby Ellis Lowe

WHEN THE MEN WERE GONE AND SHE COULD NO longer think of the word for the thing she used to light cigarettes, my grandmother, Barbara Russakoff—Bubba to those who loved her most—gave up, wrote a note, and overdosed on anti-depressants and applesauce. And it didn't work.

That was seven years ago. I was sitting in a gray cubicle in Boston pretending to work when I got the call from my mom. I don't remember the five-hour drive to Bubba's home in Skowhegan, Maine. It was strange to be in her house without her. For the first time I could remember, the large, round schoolhouse clock on the wall opposite the table was silent. When I was a kid, its tick was the constant soundtrack of summer. A few days earlier, Bubba had told my mom that it was just wound too tight and not to bother about fixing it.

We drank too much, playing cards and telling old stories. Bubba was, as far as I'm concerned, the best grandmother a kid could have. She was beautiful and wild, she smoked—as my mom explained—using each cigarette like punctuation. She played bridge and golfed, she had affairs with married men and painted her toenails coral, she made me chicken salad with sliced cucumbers, taught me to play poker and drove all over the state (speeding, with me perched on the armrest) to find the Blueberry Muffin doll I was desperate to have. She smelled like Salem Ultra Lite

100s and Jean Nate. She loved men who were unapologetic cads and told me to keep a list of people I would bite if I ever got rabies. She thought I was the best kid ever—aside from my mom. I loved her unconditionally.

And there we were in that kitchen without her. Rooting around for a bottle opener, my mom found an old grocery receipt. Bub liked to listen to the radio and write down quotes that appealed to her. In her arthritic scrawl were Mark Twain's words, "The rumors of my death have been greatly exaggerated." It was followed by a reminder to herself: "Get cigarettes."

I would have been happy if that had been the official suicide note—those were apt, hilarious instructions. Then, on her desk, I found a yellow Post-It just big enough to hold her words: "Libby, don't mourn. Be happy that I can do what I want! I love you." If Bubba had actually died, that note would have been the best thing.

When I went to see Bubba in the hospital the morning after her attempt, I thought about the year my friend's grandmother died. I was four. When my parents and I visited Maine that summer, I was worried and I asked Bubba what would happen if she died. "Oh, I'll still be your grandmother. I will just be your dead grandmother," she said easily. At the time, I was satisfied.

Bubba had been misdiagnosed with Parkinson's disease three years before her suicide attempt. Her seemingly lifelong depression became increasingly more severe. Every time I called, I wondered if it might be the last time we would speak. She'd always been vocal about her plans to kill herself when she decided the time was right. But 20 years of contradictions between her words and her actions left me simultaneously expecting her suicide and feeling sure it would never happen.

In the hospital she was in pain and very confused because the large dose of drugs had caused hallucinations. In and out of restraints, she rubbed her heels raw trying to kick her way out of the bed. Bubba couldn't move her arms much, so did the verbal equivalent of grabbing my mom by the sleeve when she mustered all her concentration to hatch a plan. "Call a cab." When my mom explained that she couldn't, Bubba archly said, "If you wouldn't be too cold, we could go sit outside on the curb and wait for the cab." Bubba is accustomed to getting her way and couldn't imagine why my mom wasn't following orders.

We're not a religious family and often find in literature what I imagine others must find in prayer. Before I left her house that weekend, I came across a passage by E. B. White that Bubba had torn out of a magazine years before and stuck on her fridge: "Hope is the thing that is left to us in a bad time. I shall get up Sunday morning and wind the clock, as a contribution to order and steadfastness." I cried. My mom rolled up her sleeves with a sigh and sadly walked over to the old clock and took it off the wall. "Well, let's get it fixed," she said, hoping as I did that maybe Bubba and the clock would find their ways back to the little brown kitchen.

They didn't. The years that followed were a mix of ups and downs, mostly downs, in various assisted living and nursing facilities. She was diagnosed with Alzheimer's, which sometimes came in handy for my mom when the staff called her about Bub's bad behavior—sleeping around, calling people bitches, the usual nursing home stuff. Blaming the Alzheimer's was much easier for us than trying to explain that Bubba would have said and done these things quite happily before she was sick—and even more happily if she knew she was pissing people off.

There was the time I brought my dog to visit, and Bub suddenly looked like a woman with an idea (or "idear" as pronounced in her thick Maine accent). She did always love a conspiracy. "Lib, could you train that dog to bite a nurse?" I got it right away: the rabies list. "It won't work. The dog's had her shots." We sat and laughed until we cried.

And the time I called and we had this phone conversation, me in Chicago, and her in home number three in Portland, Maine:

Me: Hiya Bub, how's it going over there?
Bub: I'm wearing a robe and there's a man in my bed.
Me: I hope you know him.
Bub: (Giggling) Yes, that's my boyfriend, Forrest. Your mom won't let me talk to her about my sex life.
Me: Well, I'm glad you have one again. That usually perks you up. Forrest sounds nice.
Bub: He's fine but he's no Eddie or Carl.
Me: Hmm, maybe you'll end up liking him more than you think you will.
Bub: No, I'll never care for him much, but he does take his Viagra and the sex...
Me (interrupting—who wouldn't?): Uh, that's fantastic. Just great. So, tell me about Forrest, what did he do before he landed in the nursing home?
Bub: Oh! He screwed around!! I have to go, I'm proud on you!

She always said, "I'm proud on you," rather than proud of you—my friend Bevin once pointed out that this more aggressive form of praise was actually the highest, far as she could tell.

There was the time she told my mom she had a new suicide plan: her boyfriend Ed (married) would borrow his brother's gun and shoot her. My mom, upon hearing this, couldn't help it and started laughing. Bub got mad and went into one of her rants about how she can do whatever she wants and Jack Kevorkian is a saint among men and Mother Theresa is a fucking bitch. Never mind that she herself is a non-religious Jew and saints had been of very little interest to her in the past. Then she snarled, "Well, why won't it work?" And my mom said, "Bub, Ed has Parkinson's disease! He'll never hit what he's aiming at!" In the old days, the two of them would have laughed at the absurdity of it all. But Bubba just got very sad that once again, she had no way out.

Those were the semi-funny times when she had a rotating team of what she could call boyfriends—two of whom had one leg each, one who was legally blind and many with wives—and was always after my mom to buy a double bed for her room in the home. Back then we saw a glimmer of the old Bubba, even though she kept telling us she knew she was losing her mind.

The less good days involved her crawling into my lap and crying, pleading for me to smother her with a pillow. She explained that if I loved her, I could kill her and that I was a smart girl and would not get caught—and that if I did, the sentence probably wouldn't be that long. Or her trying to get my mom to promise that when she died she would not cry and that she would leave her ashes at the cremation place for the garbage men. She didn't care that I would be known in jail as "that girl who killed her grandmother" or that my mom would be that awful woman who abandoned her mother's remains. If there had been a way for us to wish her dead, we would have because that's how much we loved her.

The last time I saw her, about two years ago, she wasn't sure who I was. I sat on her bed, she gripped my hand like there was something I could do. It felt like this was going to last forever, like it already had.

When my dad called last summer to tell me that Bubba died—from a heart attack, uncharacteristically fast and drama-free—I crumpled to the floor, sobbing, miserable and relieved. It was, at the time, a shocking emotional mix. Looking back, I imagine lots of people feel similarly when they lose someone so loved but so very ready to go.

My mom wrote a beautiful obituary about Bubba's competitive bridge skills, her humor, her strong belief in civil liberty and justice, her elegant cooking and how much she loved us all. There wasn't a funeral to attend but there was an outpouring of support.

My friend Sam credited Bubba for my irreverence. Our friend Eileen wrote to my mom, "I'm sure that she felt that the best of her was in you and Libby." My mom's cousin said Bubba taught her that apple pie is a viable breakfast option. Diane, the woman who helped my mom navigate nursing home politics and became a terrific friend to her and Bub, wrote, "She was such a hot shit!" Bevin remembered knowing her when we were little and thinking that, with her teased-up hair and her stylish bright blue Reebok high-tops, she was far too glamorous to be a grandmother.

My fiancé Erik and I went to Maine to see my parents a couple of weeks after Bub died. My mom and I had planned to scatter her ashes behind one of the granite outcroppings in my parents' yard. We'd had to give up our first choice of scattering them in the ocean because legally you can't release ashes until you're a few miles offshore. We may be from Maine but we are not marine people, so we chose the rocks at home.

In the morning, after coffee, my dad, Erik and I went out to the yard and my mom got the ashes. She poked her head out of the house and said, "Guys, I started thinking about something I'd somehow never thought about before—the wind." In addition to not being mariners, we are clumsy people. We decided that scattering could end badly. As glib as we can be sometimes, no one wanted to hear, "Hey, you have a piece of Bubba on your arm."

My dad said that he had a hydrangea ready to plant and suggested planting it on top of the ashes, so Erik dug the hole, my dad did the pouring and that was that. We spent the rest of the strange day at the beach and played some cards. Then, before dinner, my dad walked into the kitchen and said, "Well, I just watered good old Bubba." We cracked up, realizing that in a sense, we'd given her a funeral and that it was one she would have been okay with. When Erik and I went out East last summer, I checked on the plant, found myself saying, "bye, Bub" and then went to the beach. We played cards at the kitchen table, we laughed and told the old stories because we miss her. And, now that she is really gone, I got the clock out of my parents' basement and brought it home.

Libby Ellis, 33, is from Oak Park, IL and currently resides in Chicago. Her favorite Jewish holiday has always been Sukkot; her other favorite holiday is Thanksgiving. Basically, she likes food-centric events.

This essay was originally published on Oy!Chicago (www.oychicago.com).

WHO IS A JEW?: EXPLORING MY NON-KOSHER JUDAISM

By Rachel Cort

IMAGINE A YOUNG WOMAN STANDING ON A BEACH, hair long and loose. It's just past dawn. She walks into the ocean, submerging herself three times, recites a short prayer from memory, and with this small ceremony she becomes a Jew.

That woman is my mother, the year is 1979, and the beach is in Florida. She was 25 at the time and undergoing conversion shortly before her marriage to my father, a Jew by birth. I'm 25 now and only really just beginning to reflect on what it means for me that my mother is a convert. Out of respect for my mother, I won't be plumbing the depths of why she decided to convert, how she felt about it then, or how she feels about it now. She is a Jew in her community, in her heart, and in her mind. But the fact that she is a Jew by choice, not by birth, has consequences for me that I'm only beginning to grapple with.

To some people, her conversion means that I'm not really a Jew, because it was performed by a Reform rabbi. The first time I allowed the weight of that particular sentiment to really settle, it produced a sense of cognitive dissonance like I've never felt in my life. Me, not a Jew? Telling me I'm not really Jewish is like telling me that I'm not really a woman, or not really an American, or that I'm actually a towering 5'9 instead of a petite 5'1. I attended a Conservative shul growing up, was bat mitzvahed, even taught Sunday school. Right now I'm employed by a Jewish day school. While my Jewish identity doesn't necessarily stem from these things, I definitely look like a Jew on paper. And apart from my sterling Yid credentials, being Jewish has been a basic, internal fact of my identity for a long time.

My Jewishness not only anchors how I see myself, but how others see me too. Like the high school classmate who drunkenly called me a Jewish slur, or the volleyball coach who offhandedly referred to me and some of my teammates as "little Hebrews." These casual incidences of anti-Semitism didn't affect my life in a real way—I've never been subject to institutionalized anti-Semitism like quotas, for example—nevertheless they serve to remind me of the Otherness that stems from my Jewish-ness, a flexible yet impermeable membrane that sets me outside the mainstream in America. In a way, these negative incidents also serve as validating mechanisms—I have experienced, to a small degree, what other Jews throughout time have experienced, marking me as a member of the tribe.

I am a Jew in my own view and in others', yet I have to concede that there are certain parts of my life that fall outside the realm of Jewish experience because of the fact that my mother is a Jew by choice. Her side of the family, for one thing. Her family is not only Not Jewish in terms of religious affiliation, they are also Not Jewish in terms of culture, education, history, region or values. They are southern and working class, and unlike the immigrant Jews who rose above the tenements and poverty of urban centers to become a model of success in America, they have been located on a fixed spot of the socioeconomic scale for as long as they've been in America, which is probably hundreds of years. They are what I imagine when I try to think of or define "mainstream America." Their ethnicity is . . . nothing. They don't even affiliate themselves with ethnicities that were once considered to be "off-white" and still retain a dash of ethnic flavor—Irish or Italian, for example.

My mother's family is made up of intelligent, warm, funny, and kind people, but they don't fit into the traditional narrative of the Jewish people in America. My grandma makes cranberry Jello salad for Thanksgiving dinner and my grandpa collects and restores antique rifles, which he likes to occasionally fire in the woods surrounding their house. Bubbe and Zayde they are not. My brother and I are the first people on that side of the family to attend and graduate college, which I see as a manifestation of Jewish emphasis on education and learning. Not going to college is a very Not Jewish thing to do. My mother's family has been very game about attending our various b'nai mitzvot over the years, but the fact that they aren't Jewish means that they can't fully participate in or understand these rituals. I have no memories of talking about Judaism with my grandparents, wanting to spare them and myself the awkwardness of discussing the thing that separated our family.

David Hillel Gelernter writes that Jewish life has been shaped over millennia by a "cult of the family." Irving Howe described the Jewish family unit as "the living core of the community." Judaism is a covenant given to families. So what does it mean for me that half of my family has no membership in this community? Does it somehow lessen my Jewishness? I see myself in my non-Jewish family members—their noses, their sense of humor, their stubbornness—and it's like seeing a weird, *Twilight Zone* version of my non-Jewish self. Most Jews I know, surrounded by Jewish family members on both sides, lines of Jewish inheritance spanning centuries, have never had this experience. They probably haven't had the experience of attending Palm Sunday services with their cousins, either, and they almost certainly have no memories of an iron-willed, if adoring, Baptist great-grandmother.

I sometimes wonder if my fierce identification with Jewishness is an unconscious reaction to the fact that, according to some interpretations, I am not halakhically Jewish. Like most less-observant Jews, I read Ortho-dox Judaism as the "authentic" or authoritative Judaism. The fact that someone else can call into question whether or not I am Jewish is only up-setting because I, along with many other Jews, grant Orthodox Judaism that authority over me. It is also upsetting because of the fact that rabbinic Judaism recognizes matrilineal descent—if I'm not technically Jewish, then my children won't be either. Every time I see my non-Jewish family members, I am reminded of this fact. I feel my Jewishness, and the Jewishness of future generations of children and grandchildren, teeter and fall into a grey zone. I've always been frank about the fact that my mother converted, but lately I've considered whether or not to be more circumspect about sharing that information. Will the rabbis or other observant people I know reject my Jewish identity on the basis of a technicality? Rabbinic Judaism as I understand it is obsessed with the technicalities of Jewish law, so it's a very real possibility. Writing about it now feels like an "outing" of sorts. I am possessed of a double consciousness—feeling strongly Jewish, and yet acknowledging that my Judaism might not be kosher.

At 25, as I face the (as of now entirely hypothetical) prospect of marriage and children, I find myself pondering the same question that my mother surely did when she was my age—whether or not to undergo a conversion. An Orthodox one, to remove all doubt—both internal and external—about my Jewishness. I appreciate this symmetry between my mother's life and mine. And the more I ponder, the more I am grateful that her conversion has forced me to question my own Jewishness and try to locate its source. Am I Jewish because my family is? Am I not because some of them are not? Is it enough to feel like a Jew, or do I need an authority to rubber-stamp my Jewishness? Judaism is nothing if not a religion of asking questions, and these particular questions cut to the bone of one of the most important questions currently facing the Jewish community—Mi hu Yehudi? Who is a Jew?

In the end, I have decided that while I am Jewish because I was raised in a Jewish household, the fact that my mother chose to be a Jew means that I must choose to be one too. I do this now by living the Jewish values of questioning and learning. I think the conversion process, for me, would be about authenticating my Jewishness to some extent, but it would also be about the opportunity for continued learning. A basic survey of Jewish practices will show that Judaism is concerned with mindfulness, intentionality, kavannah. In a way, my mother's Reform conversion is a gift, because for me, the act of simply being a Jew is an intentional deed. I can never afford to be complacent about my Jewishness, it is an identity that I must assert and affirm over and over again. Perhaps an Orthodox conversion is a necessary part of that affirmation, and perhaps not. There's a lot I'm not sure of. One thing I am sure of: in acknowledging my mother's conversion and exploring the issues it raises for me about my own Jewishness, I have rarely felt more like a Jew. I just don't know if feeling like a Jew is enough.

> *Rachel Cort, 26, is from St. Louis, Missouri. She works at Chicago Jewish Day School where she recently refereed a dreidel-spinning competition.*

AM I A JEW-A-SAUR?

By Paul Wieder

I THINK MANY PEOPLE RELATE A PARTICULAR generation, especially ones post-PC (that's "personal computer," not "politically correct"), to its technology. For me, technology and Judaism interact at work. I began working for Chicago's Jewish Federation in 1994 after interning there while still in college. Back then, the head of the Communications Department was using a typewriter. That's a word-processing machine that has a keyboard but instead of a screen . . . you know what, just Google it. In my dorm, I used an Apple 2-e; some people have now turned these old computers into fish tanks.

During my routine at work today in 2010, I edit a website, I write for a blog, and I post the occasional podcast. All of these are related to Judaism, especially Jewish culture, in some way. I am online a great deal of the time. My job requires me to be up-to-date on every new communications trend—Facebook, Twitter, and whatever doodad they are inventing right now.

Still, in my personal Jewish life, technology has not played as large of a role. I learned my lessons from books and blackboards. I went to summer camp, where we prayed outside and sometimes slept in a tent I made from a blanket. When I went to Israel, I picked pears on a kibbutz and hiked around Jerusalem, and rode a camel in the Negev. Even while I was active in Hillel, the most advanced technology most of our programs required were copy machines (for flyers) and VCRs.

I met both my first and current wife at synagogues. At services, I wear a tallit made on a loom and a kippah my sister crocheted. There is nothing high-tech about the way I celebrate the Jewish holidays. I suppose as huts go, my succah uses advanced materials—synthetic walls, interlocking metal poles, and a bamboo roof—none of which Moses would recognize.

The same holds true for the way I impart Judaism to the next generation. I teach my kids our traditions with wax candles and manually operated toy tops and handmade breads. I teach them songs by singing, and the occasional CD. This Chanukah, I was disappointed at giving them latkes I made from a mix instead of having grated the potatoes, like my Bubbie does.

Today, my older kids play computer games and watch computer animations. But my eldest son seems to be steadily building his own city with Legos, which we bought in a store (not online) . . . while my daughter disappears into her room with her *National Geographic Kids* magazine when it arrives in the mail. I like to think this is due to my insistence that they play with battery-less toys when they were toddlers.

So, am I a Jew-a-saur, insisting on using outdated modes and technologies? And am I foisting my Luddite sensibilities (the Luddites were a group of anti-technology reactionaries who . . . or you could Google it) on my innocent kids?

Well, when our new baby was born, we ended up having to be in the hospital over Shabbat. As I had not expected this, I had not packed a siddur. So I downloaded one onto my smart phone.

Maybe there is some room in my personal Jewish life for these new-fangled gizmos, after all.

Paul Wieder, 40, was born in Cleveland, OH. He is the Public Relations Manager at the Jewish United Fund of Metropolitan Chicago. He is one of the only American critics regularly writing about Jewish music and he owns (at last count) some 400 Jewish CDs. His reviews have run in The JUF News, *Jewish papers nationally, and online. Since he began reviewing Jewish music in 1999, he has interviewed many of the performers. Recently, he has been podcasting interviews with major figures in the genre.*

WITHOUT KNOWING I HAD EVER BEEN LOST

By Eva Tuschman

I WAIT FOR THE NUMBER 60 BUS, THE EGGED LINE heading south. Through the Beersheva station young women with bleached blonde hair and miniskirts strut the walkway in plastic stilettos, past the shwarma stands and the vendors selling neon-colored toy guns and fake tattoos. The "line" for the bus is now a collection of mulling teenagers in army uniforms carrying overstuffed backpacks and M-16s slung across their shoulders. As the bus pulls up, the crowd surges toward the open door. The seats quickly fill and it doesn't seem to matter that there are no more spaces: a group of young Ethiopian girls settles in, cross-legged, in the aisle. I sit next to an older woman wearing a leopard-print blouse who proceeds to talk nervously in Russian. I somehow understand that, like me, she doesn't know where and when to get off the bus. I tell her in broken Hebrew that I don't speak Russian. She doesn't speak Hebrew.

We ride through the open desert as the driver, who navigates this surreal route everyday, speeds around every bend on the empty road. Little schoolboys with shaved heads and long twisting side-curls get on the bus and two Filipina women with a crying baby and plastic bags full of Coke bottles and bananas get off. Although there is nothing but vast desert all around, everyone seems to know their destination through this landscape of invisible pathways. A soldier stands in front of me, the barrel of his gun pointing an inch above my open-toed shoe. I slowly pull myself upright, slipping my foot under the seat.

The bus suddenly braces to a halt and the driver announces over the intercom: "Hangar Adama." As quickly as it stops, the bus skids off again— a caravan of immigrants and refugees tumbling through the open desert—and there I stand in a cloud of dust. I have seen this scene before in movies: the foreigner with the little suitcase left on the side of the road. The desert cannot help but amplify the absurd.

I've come to this failed industrial town in the Negev on the re-commendation of a Fulbright fellow who's researching contemporary dance in Tel Aviv. She gave me the phone number of her friend who's directing a dance company in an abandoned hangar. When I spoke to Lior on the phone, he ended the conversation by saying: "Most Israelis create problems. We create dance." If he was smiling on the other end of the line, I couldn't detect it.

From where I stand, there are no signs of life—the warehouses are vacant, and even the few bare trees seem to wish for their own death. Spotting a curtain flowing out of a doorway, I walk toward it, pulled closer by the steady drumbeat of what sounds like a funeral dirge.

Exactly one week ago I approached another doorway much like this one in a residential quarter of Jerusalem, but it led up a flight of stairs to an Orthodox synagogue. There was dancing there, too, though I didn't actually see it. I could hear the flamenco-like stomping and clapping of the men on the other side of the white partitions. The women, wearing headscarves, sat in folding chairs with their strollers and children, as though they were waiting in the silence of a hospital lobby.

As I part the curtain to enter, a young woman with a wild mane of wavy auburn hair and a white linen tunic runs past me and up onto a stage at the end of the long hall. She embraces another young woman in an urgent gesture of grief, and both begin to mourn what appears to be a corpse played by a fidgeting little boy. A troupe of bohemian musicians and actors lie strewn on couches, resting on each other's bodies, stretching and rehearsing songs. No one takes note of my presence.

When Lior finally appears, he gives me a tour of the hangar. His pro-fessionalism starkly contrasts with the dingy dance studios and mangy yard where there are more couches, rugs, a petting zoo with chickens and rabbits, and a native herb garden. He proudly explains that everything has not only been envisioned by his dancers but also constructed by them. My "teepee," where I am to sleep, is like a life-sized cardboard diorama, the kind I made in middle school, complete with pink stucco, exposed two-by-fours, and lopsided mobiles of yarn, twigs and pinecones.

Like all Jews who wander the desert, we eat tofu and curried mung beans and drink chai from glass jars under a canopy of palm fronds and stars. I fall asleep that night to the fading rehearsal of the elegy and awaken the next morning to the same chorus and beating of the drum. In the first class, a young woman named Orit leads us in sensory-awareness exercises. As we roll around the carpet, we are told to imagine floating on a cloud, peacefully balancing in mid-air. Suddenly, there is a loud sound of an airplane's engine overhead, followed by echoing booms. No one seems to notice as, eyes closed, they continue to roll on their clouds to Orit's melodic voice.

A few days ago, I was lying on a beach chair in North Tel Aviv watching old ladies inch carefully deeper into the Mediterranean. I wondered how many of them were survivors and how many miles from this glorious sprawl of sunbathing teens gunfire and suffering—the stuff of common news—occurred in real time. Across the pure blue sky, fighter jets swerved to landing pads nearby. Boys continued to play paddle ball in the sand while their girlfriends shut their eyes against the sun.

In the hangar, I open my eyes to see Orit standing above me. "I'm sorry," I say. "I don't understand what to do."

"You should really learn Hebrew," she responds in English. "It is, after all, our language."

I am still getting used to the idea that I am part of the "our" to whom she refers. Since arriving in Israel, I have found myself staring at strangers in shopping malls and cafés, wondering what an Iraqi-Polish waiter has in common with a Moroccan grocery clerk or a Bulgarian taxi driver. Judaism has suddenly become a perplexing term as its representatives pass before me in every possible color and from every culture the world over. How, after thousands of years, did they all end up reunited together in this strange desert? I'm not even ready to begin considering how I fit into this enthralling mosaic.

That night the dancers congregate following Lior's lead in several cooperative exercises. At a certain point there is a linguistic cue, which I miss, that the directives are over as people begin to move freely to the sinuous sounds of an oud. Everyone dances alone, yet there is a synergy across the floor as each person enters into a private flow of expression: A pale redheaded girl spins in circles while an olive-skinned man with a raven ponytail swivels his hips and sways from side to side. I suddenly feel, amid the whirl of movement, like I am an animal who has come upon its herd without knowing I had ever been lost. All night I pretend to dance, but really I am watching them dance, watching their faces, believing they have been living secret magical lives all these years without me.

The last note of the oud disappears and with it, the dancers retreat into the night. Before tucking into my teepee, I drink tea with a soldier on short-term leave from his base. In his thick Russian accent he tells me: "If you learn one thing about Israel remember this: We are an army with a country. Not a country with an army."

Next year many of Lior's dancers will be practicing different routines, but their costumes will be near identical: green or tan fatigues and felt berets with plastic pendants pinned on. They will learn to stand upright in straight lines, to memorize patterns of running and ducking through desert terrain, and they will be trained to aim and shoot a combat rifle. All culture is ultimately a matter of choreography. For now, though, they continue to twirl on trapezes, sew their own tunics and lounge tranquilly late into the night playing Bedouin drums and smoking cigarettes under the stars.

Eva Tuschman was born in the San Francisco Bay Area and is an alumna of Stanford University, where she earned a degree in Cultural and Social Anthropology. As a freelance writer, she has produced texts for several ethnographic projects, the last of which included oral-histories of Jewish Israeli refugees from the Middle East. Her publications have appeared in New York Jewish Week's Text/Context, *and she was also a principal contributor to the* Tassajara Dinners and Desserts *cookbook, after having cooked for several years at the well-known Zen Buddhist monastery and retreat center in Big Sur, California. Eva has a background in visual arts and modern dance, and is currently completing a Master's degree in Clinical Psychology.*

This essay was originally published in The Jewish Week's Text/Context *and is excerpted from the anthology* What We Brought Back: Jewish Life After Birthright, *edited by Wayne Hoffman and produced by Nextbook Inc. and Birthright Israel NEXT, and most recently in the anthology* The Best Women's Travel Writing of 2011.

CONVERSION OF COMFORT

By Rachel Wright

I'VE BEEN TOLD GOING THROUGH THE JEWISH conversion process with a loved one would at times make me question my own Jewish upbringing. This last year and a half I was blessed to be a part of my boyfriend Ryan's path to discovering his own identity as he became a Jew by choice—and turns out, I learned a lot about my own Jewish identity as well.

At first, I approached Ryan's conversion differently than other couples that have gone through this experience. Instead of going with him to each Introduction to Judaism class, attending study sessions with our rabbi, I watched him do it alone. For those of you wondering, this was not out of laziness, or too-recent memories of watching the clock tick during my own Jewish education as a teenager. It was merely because I wanted to sit on the sidelines, and let him find Judaism independently.

For Ryan, conversion was not an act out of respect to a Jewish girl he loved. It was not because I set boundaries about my own Jewish expectations. His conversion was about a man taking his own path to serve under the God of Israel.

Ryan's decision to convert was one made on his own. He decided to do this, and I encouraged him to take this journey alone. It was very important to me that Ryan define the Jew he would become on his own. Our Jewish future as a couple will be defined later. So on Monday, the

6th of Elul 5770 (August 16, 2010), Ryan made his covenant to God and converted. Going through a Conservative rabbi at our synagogue, Ryan met before a beit din (rabbinical court), went through the traditions of hatafat dam brit (circumcision—yes, ouch!) and concluded with submersion in the mikvah (bath used for the purpose of ritual immersion).

As the rabbi blessed my boyfriend with his Hebrew name—Israel David—the tears in Ryan's eyes as he lowered his head to be blessed in our traditional manner made the event more powerful than I had anticipated.

"5771 will be your year," the rabbi spoke to Ryan as we concluded. "This will truly be your New Year, as will all the High Holiday seasons be for the rest of your life."

The power in this statement was immense. I may not have attended one class with him over the last year and a half, but it suddenly felt like he was at every Sunday school class with me as a child and was on the "inside" to all of my summer camp jokes from decades ago. This man was now going share a meaningful holiday with me.

My sudden struggle was how I would define "meaningful." What would be different this year?

Ryan hasn't missed a beat when explaining to his non-Jewish family the customs we practice. Admittedly, we don't follow all the laws, but we do try to be "good" Jews. We light Shabbat candles every week together, and share intense passions towards tikkun olam (repairing the world). We live as Jewish people with our hearts and minds open to the will of God.

This year, Ryan suggested we open our hearts by closing off our electronic link to the outside world and leaving our cell phones turned to off for Shabbat. Just as we were turning onto the road to line up to park at services, I heard Ryan on his phone with his parents explaining our disconnect for the next 24 hours.

Now, it's cliché to make jokes about one's own affliction with their cell phone. I deem mine as moderately inappropriate. I don't sleep with it next to my pillow (anymore) and I've been weaned from keeping it in my lap while I drive. Services however? It is off. I can go two hours without a text message. But for a full day? This was not something I was ready to do.

Kol Nidre services are my favorite. I love the melodies, the chanting, the solemn pounding on the chest. "I have done wrong. I beg for forgiveness." Somewhere in between the standing and sitting relays I also enjoy the walk to the bathroom where quick "hellos" and "good yontif" can be whispered. This year, as I made my way to the ladies room, I did see something shocking—three girls hanging out by the main lobby texting on their cell phones. Now I understood Ryan's comment about leaving the world out of this very solemn day.

I am not judging these young girls for following their own rules for the holiday. As I reflect on my own discipline of this past Yom Kippur, I was not entirely strict about my phone. I was way more conscious of its use, and even felt guilty after I absentmindedly updated my Facebook status before Ne'ilah service to tell all of my friends I was hungry. But, I did atone immediately—talk about under the wire!

Maybe Ryan, so new in his Jewish world, understood something I had forgotten. The High Holidays are a time to renew, evaluate and repent. To be aware of all the roles I play—girlfriend, best friend, daughter, sister and stranger to all those who don't know me. It is a time to improve in all these facets, and next year commit to not allowing the distractions of daily luxuries to compete with this.

When Yom Kippur ended, food consumed, and my blood sugar raised as the battery charged on my BlackBerry, I concluded with a New Year's resolution to be more open to the holiness of the holidays and the laws that come with them.

Through Ryan's conversion I was reminded of the loveliness of Judaism as we now begin to build our Jewish customs and laws to discuss and choose to follow together. It's much better than being on two separate teams.

Rachel Wright is a 30-year old rockin' Detroiter who isn't afraid to yell from the rooftops her passion for her hometown. When not attending a Jewish non-profit fundraising event, she's usually sitting on some sort of Jewish non-profit conference call—which is especially enjoyable to her employer who enables her high level of involvement. When not volunteering, Rachel works in the health insurance arena, at her family's national Pharmacy Benefit Manager saving people money throughout the country. Her new venture is a corporate social-action endeavor. Rachel was never married to Sean Penn, can occasionally be caught with cat hair on her clothes, and would likely beat you on the tennis court.

This essay was originally published on www.nextgenJews.org.

WE LIVE IN LOVING MEMORIES

By Inbal Freund

IN MEMORY OF NOAM MAYERSON, MY STEP COUSIN who fell in the Lebanon war, my cousin Chani Dikshtein, her husband Yossi and their child, Shuvael, who were shot to death on their way to spending Shabbat with friends. This is also in memory of older loved ones: Shlomo Gabriel Freund, my father's brother who gave his life while defending Gush Etzion in 1948, and my grandmother's brother, David Metal, who fell while commanding his troops in the south on the same year. Further, I would like to commemorate my grandfather's siblings and parents who perished in the Holocaust. May their memories be blessed and guide us to meaningful growth and much joy of life in our present and future days.

A. My father.
My father has good eyes, which have seen a lot. He has grey hairs that sometimes sneak out in mischievously boyish wisps from under his kippa. He has wrinkled hands with blessed old age stains, which treat every flower in his garden with great gentleness.

On Rosh Hashanah, my father's big hands open the Torah scroll at the synagogue. Full of emotion, his voice trembles above the crowd, reading from Jeremiah, chapter 31—the consolation prophecy describing the return to Zion. Embedded in that glory lies our foremother

Rachel's great agony for her lost sons—the ones who perished during the journey to Israel, and never made it to the Promised Land. When the reading is over, the cantor blesses Yonatan, son of Rachel and Moshe. My father's good eyes are lit with splendor and laughter as he steps quietly down from the Bimah back into the crowd.

In the army, my father's role was taking care of the dead. His job was to bring them to a dignified Jewish burial. He never tells us anything of his past actions; he is not a man of many words. Until today, whenever somebody passes away in my old hometown, my father vanishes for a few hours to help treat the dead. It's called "Chesed Shel Emet"—the benevolence of righteousness. Unlike his parents' generation who built the institutions of our country and set up its main structures, his Chesed is quiet and responsive to the events that happen around him.

Sometimes I wonder how my quiet father can carry all that weight on his shoulders.

B. Masoret—tradition.

> Moses received the Torah from Sinai and passed it on to Joshua, Joshua to the Elders; the Elders to the Prophets; and the Prophets passed it on to the Men of the Great Assembly . . .
> —*Pirkey Avot*

The generations that came before us are embedded within us. They escort us as we celebrate our holidays. On Yom Kippur or at university graduation, their eyes are watching, examining our actions, giving advice and meaning to mundane life. We are expected to relate to them. The glory of their memories commands us to better the world. To improve what they have given us. To carry their greatness to our inheritance. To create the next part of the chain, day by day.

I study what my forefathers studied. I study what my foremothers did not always have access to. I have the freedom to wander around beloved texts, I have the freedom to walk in ancient pathways. I live in a world which reinvents itself with every passing day, where technology dictates an ever growing pace of life. I live in the liminal space between old and new as I try to make my own way forward.

C. National Memorial Day 2007
A frantic rush. It is 10:30am and I'm running up the mountain. It's hot and I feel heavy. I'm running to be there on time for the ceremony, to stand

next to my father when the siren that traditionally marks Memorial Day will begin to pierce our ears with memories.

It's crowded and hot. The cemetery is flooded with people swarming in from every direction. They are dressed in blue and white; some wear only one color: black.

I run. I smile with gratitude at teenagers who wear their youth movements' uniform as they hand me flowers to put on a grave. However, I refuse their offer, as well as the water bottles that soldiers provide for the vast crowd. For now, I run forward with the crowds.

It feels just like before a big pilgrimage. I see visions of a white river of people who are rushing towards the Wailing Wall to read the Book of Ruth on the holiday of Shavuot. Before dawn kisses the sky which lies above it, darkness is broken with a new light.

I stop. I got too high. From this standpoint, I can see my family members trying to find their way to each other. They move in the crowd, not aware of how close they really are to each other. The focal point is Noam's grave. I witness the strong quiet presence of his parents and some of his siblings. They are all standing, ready for the ceremony. I see familiar heads everywhere. The only islands in the crowd are the graves.

I locate my father. He is standing down there, trying to gently push his way forward. I can imagine his debate with himself; whether to further protect his head from the burning sun, as I see him put his funny-looking hat over his kippah. It's 11am. My father's big hand freezes in the air as the siren blows.

We stand and stare at the ground. New beloved ones have been buried here this year. In my mind I try to remember each of my family members who are commemorated today in the short two-minute period. I'm left overwhelmed.

The ceremony is over. We unite under the big tree we have come to know in the past year on our visits here. Our tribe members gather. My cousin's wife, Hadassah, is 15 days late in her pregnancy; both of her beautiful blond-haired daughters run around. We all hug and kiss and fill each other in on latest news. I take Noa, Noam's new niece, in my arms. She is a beautiful two-month-old baby. She is life. I say shalom to Noam's fiancé, not really knowing what to say to her lovely enigmatic smile.

A man who rescued Noam's body from the tank is standing between us all. Wrapped in our family, he is telling of the rescue efforts. The children run around and we are hiding from the sun behind a tree, behind sunglasses, all attuned to his story. We are embraced by the tree's shade; we are embraced by this man's story. We embrace him back.

The clock is ticking and we start to depart. People are going to Noam's parents' house to be together. With my father and others the ascent up the mountain begins. We make our way to the next ceremony, which should be taking place at 1 p.m., on top of the mountain. My father sneaks apples to our handbags; the day is hot and long. We are all encouraging each other to drink. The sun beats down on our heads; there is still much to be done.

There is heavy security on the way to the terror victim's ceremony. The main speaker is the Prime Minister. We wander on and on in a labyrinth of blue plastic cloth, passing through different guard points to get in to the central ceremony. Our agony is our passport on this journey. We mourn for my cousin Chani, her husband Yossi and their child Shuvael, who were shot five years ago. It's 12:45 p.m. and we are afraid of being late. We start running again in the roads that lead up, passing by the tombs of Herzl's children as we go further on our way to be with Chani's nine living orphans.

The Talmud says, "Everyone who visits takes away one-sixtieth of the illness." My father runs to support my cousins, to take his part.

We get there; see our family members in the distance, by the stage. We listen to the cantor crying a prayer of mourning, "El Male Rachamim," once more and then withdraw back down the mountain to make it to the next ceremony; the hour of 1:30 p.m. is drawing near.

I run. I try to locate the shortest and quickest way to go down this mountain, to the Gush Etzion ceremony. To show my father the way. His brother is buried there, Rachel's son who never made it to the Promised Land. It has been exactly 59 years of independence and loss for my father. I stand with him at the mass grave, nodding my head to greet more of the elders of our family. I kiss my twin brother, who was named after our fallen uncle. The memorial service begins. El Male Rachamim again. We stand on both sides of our father. We embrace him as his body leans towards the earth.

D. Independence Day

The sad, heavy, choking, patched blanket of ceremonies is lifted. We can never really take some pieces back as we return to our homes to prepare for our Independence Day. The shift is so dramatic. Like a transformation from a long fast to the festive joy of Purim. Like a great light that blinds eyes which dwelled in much darkness. By the evening, the sky is lit with fireworks. My head is still pounding from the sun. From the distance the fireworks sound like shots, and I have to look up to remember that this is an expression of joy, which is not taken for granted. It's an expression of freedom.

My forefathers are looking down at us, seeing good, old, stained hands caress our heads. My father's soft eyes are full of light.

Inbal Freund-Novick, 31, is an organizational consultant and co-founder of "The Unmasked Comics Project," a social change comics venture with comics artist Chari Pere. Inbal has been recently director of Mavoi Satum, a Jerusalem-based organization dedicated to solving the social injustice faced by mesoravot get (women denied religious divorces) and helping those in need until Israeli and halachic legal solutions are determined. As a 2006-07 Legacy Heritage (Wexner) Fellow at The Jewish People Policy Institute, Inbal studied Young Jewish Leadership, focusing on the generational gap between the institutional Jewish world and the younger generation. Previously, Inbal founded and directed Chaverim, a Jewish Studies learning community for new immigrants and Israelis on campuses across Israel. A founding steering committee member of PICZ: the Presentense Institute for Creative Zionism, Inbal has also been Kol Dor conference Co-Chair for year 2007 and is currently the head of the interfaith dialogue task force of the World Jewish Diplomatic Corps. Inbal has also taught Hebrew and Jewish Studies in Manchester, England. In her free time, Inbal is a published poet with the "Mashiv Haruach" Jewish poets company and a member of the Yakar Beit Midrash and choir. She loves taking long walks in Jerusalem streets with Yoel, her husband.

This essay was originally published in Jewlicious *as part of the 60 Bloggers project, a co-production of Jewlicious.com, and the* Let My People Sing Festival *published daily for 60 days to celebrate Israel's 60 birthday.*

FEEDING MY JEWISH SOUL

By Kate Bigam

I'VE ALWAYS BEEN JEWISH.

Well, kind of.

I grew up in suburban Ohio, where I was the only Jewish student in a high school of 2,000. Perhaps unsurprisingly, my mom and I comprised 100 percent of the local Jewish population, members of a congregation two cities away that held Shabbat services twice a month because there weren't enough Jews in the area to generate weekly interest. My bat mitzvah was held at the country club because our tiny church-cum-synagogue didn't have the capacity—or the air conditioning!—to accommodate my large August service. Upon receipt of the invitation, my friends' parents called to inquire what a bat mitzvah was: "Will they carry Kate around in a chair, like in the movies?"

I know what you're thinking: Oy gevault.

Don't get me wrong: I've always felt Jewish. My mother instilled in me Jewish values from the time I was young, even when we were putting up a Christmas tree with my secularly Protestant father. Despite my surroundings—and perhaps because of them—I've always felt deeply connected to my (somewhat amorphous) Jewish identity. It didn't matter that we didn't know many other Jews, my mom told me, because I was blessed with "a Jewish soul." And that, she said, mattered most.

Cut to college when, blindsided by the pain of an ex-boyfriend's suicide, I renewed my spiritual relationship with my childhood rabbi in an attempt to cope. At age 20, I'd all but forgotten about my Jewish soul, save the occasional High Holiday service with my mother. But life had thrown me for a loop, and it was going to take more than another frat party to heal me. My rabbi never said it directly, but her advice was clear: Why not (re)connect with my Judaism?

And that's how I found myself in Washington, D.C., an eager but wary participant in the Religious Action Center of Reform Judaism's work/study summer program for college students. As excited as I was for a new undertaking, to call my initial experience "culture shock" would be to make a colossal understatement. My fellow participants came from infinitely-more-Jewish-than-me backgrounds—some were alumni of Jewish camps and youth groups I'd never heard of, or board members of their campus Hillels; still others were aspiring rabbis, a professional aspiration that seemed entirely foreign to me.

I, meanwhile, struggled to keep up with my new friends, floundering through the names of Jewish holidays and failing to understand the baffling Hebrew slang they used in casual conversation. I'd never heard half of the prayers they knew by heart (notably, the lengthy Birkat), and—GASP!—I'd never traveled to Israel, as most of them had. It was clear to us all that I wasn't as up on my Judaism as they were ("You're practically Lutheran," one semi-joked), but I was determined to prove that Jews come from all backgrounds, that Judaism isn't about how you're raised but how you feel. Multiple times per day, I reminded myself that I belonged there just as much as my peers did, clinging to my mother's insistence that I bore a Jewish soul.

There were some tears (please see aforementioned reference to "practically Lutheran"), but I stuck it out. The program placed me into an internship with a civil rights organization that advocated for same-sex couples and their families, where the rainbow-streaked sticker on my desk read, "My faith makes me a gay rights activist." It was a sentiment with which I was proud to align: Who needs hymns and Hebrew when there's social justice to pursue? Finally, I'd found something Jewish that I could connect to, no foreign language skills or trips to Israel required. Invigorated and inspired, I threw myself into my work, and I vowed to continue to it even when I'd left the program—to remain both an activist and an active Jew long after my time in D.C. came to a close.

On that last night, when my fellow program participants and I went around a circle and described aloud how our experiences had affected us,

I could hardly put my transformation to words. That summer changed my life for the better, and in very lasting ways. Five years later, I've since cultivated a full and distinctly Jewish life in the capital, where I moved after graduation—to work for a Jewish nonprofit, no less!—and I continue to discover my Judaism every day, falling in love with this age-old faith and the culture and the community it provides. I'm pleased to discover I use distinctly Yiddish phrases with regularity (OK, mostly just "Mazel tov"); I feel guilty when I eat bacon, though I'll likely never abandon it; I read *Tablet* and *Jewlicious* and keep up with Jewish current events. But it's about more than that: I feel my Judaism most strongly in holiday celebrations with friends, in shared experiences with other young Jewish professionals, and in my involvement with organizations, Jewish and otherwise, that tackle the social justice issues that speak to my values.

Of course, sometimes I'm just that same small-town girl who doesn't know the hymns or the Hebrew words or a single line of that pesky Birkat—but the enormity of the ways in which I've grown far outnumber those little things that have stayed the same. When I first began this journey, displaced and more than a little confused, I never dreamed where the experience would take me—into adulthood, into my Judaism, and, as a result, into myself. My mom was right: This is who I am. And Christmas tree or not, my Jewish soul is thriving.

Kate Bigam is a 26-year old blogger who recently returned to Ohio after three years in Washington, DC, where she worked for the Reform Jewish Movement. Though currently between jobs (read: unemployed), there's a bright spot: She'll be traveling to Israel for the first time in 2011!

A version of this essay was originally published on RJ.org.

A NEW KIND OF JEWISH GEOGRAPHY

By Perry Teicher

WE ALL INSTINCTIVELY KNOW THAT JEWS ARE SPREAD across the world, but when we run into Jewish communities in what feel like unlikely places, we are still somewhat surprised. For over two years while in the Peace Corps in Kazakhstan and traveling throughout Central Asia and the Caucuses, I became a part of a Jewish community far from home and explored Jewish communities in an often forgotten corner of the world.

While I joined Peace Corps to move beyond my comfort zone and have the opportunity to make a difference, my experience in the Michigan Jewish community helped propel me to pursue this path. My involvement with Hillel at the University of Michigan, BBYO in high school, and Adat Shalom Synagogue growing up helped me develop an interest in social activism. The Jewish community is a model of supporting those in need. From a young age, we encourage students to take responsibility for their actions and try to instill the idea of tikkun olam. Through community organization, the community provides a structure for those who want to volunteer. As a leader in these organizations, I saw the challenges involved in building and sustaining community and the benefits of inspiring others to take responsibility.

KAZAKHSTAN

Judaism has always been an important part of my life, so when I moved to Kazakhstan with Peace Corps, I naturally reached out to the Jewish community. I had read there were around 30,000 Jews across the country, the ninth largest by land mass in the world. Given the physical size of the country, that's not a lot of Jewish citizens. Most Jews are located in Almaty, the former capital, and home of two Chabad congregations. After three months of training in a nearby town, I shipped off to a provincial capital 43 hours by train across the country—Aktobe.

I arrived in the middle of winter. Night fell at 6 p.m. and it didn't lift until 10 a.m. That's a tough environment to move into, especially when I had only just begun to learn Russian. I had learned about the Jewish community during training and I had exchanged a few phone calls in broken Russian with the one observant Jew in Aktobe, Ya'akov. Chanukah was just around the corner, so I was invited to the community Chanukah dinner.

I was ushered to the middle of the table, to an empty seat across from a woman who spoke a little English. It was mainly an older crowd, with one couple in their 30s and a 12-year-old boy. The food was kosher, although only Ya'akov kept kosher (a situation that proved interesting as I transported kosher meat between Almaty to Aktobe later in my service). Although not lit, a Chanukiah sat on the counter as a reminder of the holiday.

After eating platefuls of kosher plouf (a Central Asian rice dish), the woman across from me began to sing. She began with "Tum Balalaika," then I jumped in with "Chanukah, O Chanukah," then we sang along with "Yerushalayim Shel Zahav." Despite my unmelodic voice, our harmony came together across languages.

I later learned from a Jewish Book Day celebration that more Jewish children live in Aktobe. Many of these children, however, are just warming up to their Jewish identity. Aktobe, only 30 kilometers from the Russian border, was a destination during and after World War II for Jews transported from Russia proper and Europe.

My connection with the Jewish community deepened after this first dinner, but it was this event that I most often recall. I still remember the mushroom salads and baked fish. There was nothing on the table that we would consider traditional Chanukah food in America. Chanukah, as a community event, was felt to be a traditionally important Jewish holiday.

Jewish education had only recently restarted since the fall of the Soviet Union. The younger generation knows more about Judaism than their grandparents, but is unable to put it into a broader context. As the first generation in decades to grow up Jewish, the younger generation is putting together the bigger picture through a world very different than their parents and grandparents.

TURKMENISTAN

Sitting in a yurt in a village of 200 people in the middle of the Karakum desert was not the place I expected to be introduced to the Turkmenistan Jewish community. After completing two years of Peace Corps service in Kazakhstan and working extensively with the Jewish community, I spent four months traveling around Central Asia. I made an effort to meet with the Jewish community in every country, but in Uzbekistan was told that the head of the Turkmenistan Jewish community was out of the country on vacation. They gave me his contact information but noted there would be no reason to call. More so, I was warned that organized Judaism occupies an illegal position in the country's laws. As I had to be with a guide through my Turkmenistan trip, I decided there would be no point in trying to get in touch.

Back to the yurt. We had only crossed the border from Uzbekistan into Turkmenistan a day earlier. But, we already felt very close to our guide, a wonderful ethnic Russian man, from Turkmenistan. That's what happens when you spend 24 hours together with someone, driving through the desert. That night, we had been drinking and we started talking about jeans—Levi Jeans. As I hadn't talked or thought about jeans in a couple years, I had trouble pronouncing "Levi," and mixed it up with "Levy." Oleg, our guide, asked about my background.

While I usually was upfront with my Judaism, since I really did not know Oleg and since I was told to be particularly careful with Judaism in Turkmenistan, it took another shot to get "Jewish" out of my mouth. Oleg, clearly amused that I found it difficult to say I was Jewish, followed-up with "my best friend is Jewish!" I decided to go on a limb, "Is his name Zinovi?" I say as I pull out my phone. Our guide's best friend is the head of the Jewish community in Turkmenistan, and was back in town. Small world barely describes this experience—this was Jewish geography at its finest.

AZERBAIJAN

In America, we usually focus on large divisions within the Jewish community—Ashkenazic, Sephardic, and Mizrachi, and more often Reform, Conservative, and Orthodox. Through traveling, I was introduced to a much wider range of Jewish communities. An American Azeri friend told me I should go visit the Mountain Jews in Azerbaijan. I thought he was joking. I had first been introduced to the Mountain Jews through *Absurdistan*, by Gary Shteyngart. How could they be real? A week after arriving in Baku, I took a four-hour bus ride and arrived in Quba, the home of the largest community of Mountain Jews in the former Soviet Union. The city is divided into two parts—the Jewish part (Krasnaya Sloboda) and the Muslim part (Quba).

A Peace Corps volunteer in the city had wanted to explore Krasnaya Sloboda since arriving in Azerbaijan, so we crossed the bridge into what is considered the last completely Jewish settlement outside Israel. If you did not know everyone was Jewish, you would have no idea people weren't Muslim Azeri. Then, you look up and see Jewish stars and Hebrew text on every other building. We wandered through the streets, and found the one functioning synagogue. Like many Jewish communities in small towns, there was a clear demographic shift; mainly only young kids and the elderly. Young adults and middle-age men seem to have largely left. It's a similar problem, but exacerbated, that we have in many American cities—if there's no opportunity, you leave when you can.

AMERICA

Through my travels, I've learned that we experience a much easier Judaism in America than overseas. It's relatively easy to switch or hide identities in America. Our ethnicity isn't on our passports and more so, Judaism is generally recognized as a mix of ethnic, religious, and national factors. While traveling, I was first considered an American and then Jewish. I grew up in a warm, welcoming, and inspiring Jewish community, but it was while traveling and spending time with Jewish communities overseas that I gained a better perspective on my own Jewish identity.

When I signed up for Peace Corps, I noted that due to my co-curricular activities, it would be very clear I am Jewish. I thought of this identity as relatively established—I would learn more about myself but my understanding of Judaism would likely not change dramatically while living overseas and presumably having little Judaic interaction. During the two and a half years in Central Asia, however, I gained insight into my conception of religion and community. I organized a Seder in Russian, prayed alongside Jewish students in Tashkent Hillel who actively chose to be identify as Jewish, and listened to a Jewish woman in a small Dushanbe apartment explain staying in Tajikistan despite a bloody civil war outside her door in order to continue to help her community survive. Returning to America two and a half years later, while my Judaism may be less visible on my resume, I have a much better understanding of global Judaism and my connection with my belief.

Perry Teicher, 25, from West Bloomfield, MI, is pursuing a JD/MBA and a career in social entrepreneurship. While traveling through Central Asia and the Caucuses, he often transported kosher meat between Almaty and Aktobe, a distance of over 1,000 miles. He was the 2010-2011 Repair the World Fellow at Repair the World.

A version of this essay was printed in the Detroit Jewish News.

NOSH, DAVIN, KVELL OR EAT, PRAY, LOVE THE WEST SIDE WAY

By Angela Himsel

LEEBA RIVKA GILBERSTEIN IS 27 YEARS OLD, FIVE pounds overweight, (okay, maybe 10), spiritually numb, and single. Every nosh of the home-baked challah bread that her girlfriends have recently learned to make in the challah-baking craze that's swept the upper West Side of Manhattan has shown up on her hips. She can davin the shemoneh esreh, the silent prayers comprised of 18 blessings, in Hebrew quicker than anyone, though rapid repetition has rendered her anesthetized to their meaning. Leeba Rivka has posted her profile (kvelling, albeit in a measured and modest manner: Modern Orthodox woman, educated, outgoing, healthy, thank G-d, loves museums, art documentaries and books on Jewish history, especially Holocaust-themed...) on sawyouatsinai.com, frumster.com and even, heaven forefend, that most secular of Jewish dating sites, JDate.com, in search of her beshert, her soulmate. Jewish legend has it that every Jew in the world actually stood at Mt. Sinai with his or her soul mate when the Ten Commandments were given. Now, the trick was to find the one she "saw at Sinai."

Leeba Rivka hates being a part of the "Jewish singles' crisis," as if, within the scope of modern-day afflictions, she's right up there with North Korea's nuclear program. She wishes she could be more like her friend Shoshana who just left for a six month stint at a women's seminary in Israel, with the stated purpose to come back engaged or, G-d willing, married. The rabbis there take it upon themselves to fix the young people up, no mitmazel.com necessary. Begrudgingly, Leeba Rivka admires Shosh for treating her single state like an illness that needs to be cured, or like she's unemployed and is seeking full-time employment, systematically and thoroughly and unsentimentally.

It's the middle of a hot summer, and the fall High Holidays and the frenetic synagogue-hopping and furtive eye-catching that they entail are looming menacingly. Leeba Rivka decides she needs a break from the Modern Orthodox Jewish dating world in New York City, and maybe with some perspective she will eat less noodle kugel and lose five pounds (10?), reconnect to more meaningful prayer and learn to love and kvell at everything life offers, not just her one-year-old nephew's recent achievement, "Oy, you made in the potty, you cutie!" The 10 day cruise to Greece, Turkey, Israel and Egypt looks great but is outside her budget. She is quite tempted by the kosher Eastern European trip: the Warsaw Ghetto, Auschwitz, Birkenau. A friend of hers had gone there on her honeymoon and loved it, but it's expensive. Finding one's own authentic neshama (soul) requires a lot of money.

There's notyourtypicalweekend.com, which she'd done once, and while the broad palette of diversions, including life coaches, yoga and ropes courses, as well as the ever-present presence of a rabbi who delivered Talmudic talks on the Temple and the meaning of the red heifer, had been a nice change, Leeba Rivka has had more than a few moments when she'd thought: Jews on ropes courses, clutching their yarmulkahs, holding up their skirts, who are they trying to be, goyim?

Club Getaway in the Berkshires looks far more doable, a kosher weekend under strictest rabbinical supervision (the food, not the activities), a lot of kibbetzing, music on Saturday night at the close of the Sabbath . . . it's like summer camp for Jewish professionals. But the thought of being charming and entertaining for an entire weekend, of judging and being judged on her level of religious observance (Leeba Rivka wears pants, on occasion, and she eats in non-kosher restaurants, albeit only cold vegetarian items!) seems like more of a tzuris (a headache) than a simcha (a joyous occasion).

She doesn't have enough money for a thorough, neshama-searching journey that will take her through concentration camps or across the Mediterranean, and she has a terrible aversion to an entire weekend eating over-salted beef teriyaki that bears an uncanny resemblance to brisket, and speed dating with nudnick Shloimeys who have jobs doing something in computers and pride themselves on their shuckeling (swaying) during prayer.

So, when she hears about the Tu B'Av celebration sponsored by a local Chabad group, she figures why not?

Leeba Rivka is only vaguely familiar with Tu B'Av. It's a minor, post-Biblical holiday that takes place in the summer on the 15th of the Jewish month of Av. Back in the days of the Second Temple in Jerusalem, Tu B'Av was the time of the wood offering, and was quite the happening festival. Coinciding with the full-moon, it connoted love and romance and fertility, and today is feted as the Jewish Valentine's Day. But who cares about its history? Far more important, there's a Tu B'Av singles party downtown on the roof of a club called Splashtop and it only costs $15.

Leeba Rivka shows up in a white, flowing dress (Everyone is asked to wear all white—apparently, back in the day, this was so that the rich couldn't be distinguished from the poor, but in today's world, white shows off Leeba Rivka's suntan very nicely). There's only hummus and vegetables and a few other low-caloric offerings, so she doesn't eat too much, which is good. She sings Hebrew prayers and sways with her eyes closed atop a tall building in New York City with a view of the Hudson River, and feels as if she's connecting to God more than she does during her daily prayers. Then, she gazes into the Reflection Pool and sees the face of a handsome, dark-haired, dark-skinned young man clad in white shirt and white jeans.

His name is Roni, he just got out of the Israeli army, and is doing a round-the-world trip in search of himself. He'd hooked up with Chabad, famous for its outreach and for accepting Jews of all stripes and types. The rabbi is on record as saying that he'll perform the wedding for free for any couple that meets through their events. When their eyes meet in the pool, schmaltzy and sentimental as it sounds, it's Love.

Six years younger than Leeba Rivka, and a secular, Yemenite Jew from a Kibbutz in the Galilee, Roni is not someone Leeba would have chosen or who would have chosen her on any of the dating websites. But when it turns out they've seen the same documentaries—*Was Picasso Jewish?*— and read many of the same books—*I Grew Up With Mice and Lice: a Memoir of a Hidden Child in Poland in World War II* Leeba recognizes him as the one she saw at Sinai.

The sequel to *Nosh, Davin, Kvell* is *Shtup, Schluff, Kvetch* (Sex, Sleep, Complain), a portrayal of Leeba's subsequent marriage to Roni. The early years.

Angela Himsel grew up as a Christian in Jasper, Indiana and converted to Judaism many years ago. Her fiction and non-fiction have appeared in many magazines and newspapers, including the New York Times, the Forward, the Jewish Week, Lilith, Partisan Review, BOMB, *and online at* beliefnet.com *and* ducts.org. *She currently writes the Rockower-Award winning column, "Ange-tevka," for* Zeek.net, *where she's mulled everything from caffeine suppositories on Yom Kippur to the proto-Sinaitic alphabet and its connection to her great-niece's name. She is 49-years-old, and lives in New York City with her husband and three children. She recently completed a novel,* God on the Couch, *in which God is undergoing psychoanalysis.*

This essay was originally published in Zeek.

THE GODFATHER

By Alyssa Latala

WE HAD BEEN DATING FOR SIX MONTHS WHEN I decided it was time for Joe and I to have "the talk." We sat on his couch for a long time, going through the familiar pattern of "What's wrong?" and "Nothing" and silence before I was able to spit it out.

"I want to raise my children Jewish."

What a load to lay on the new (Catholic) boyfriend. I skipped right through the talk of getting married and jumped right ahead to the babies. And not only was I bringing up our future children, I was asking him to commit to making Jewish babies. I figured I'd be logging onto JDate when I got home.

But Joe surprised me that night. He had already given the topic a lot of thought.

Joseph John Latala III, graduate of St. Raymond's elementary school and Marquette University, committed to raising a Jewish family.

We got engaged a year later. We participated in inter-faith group sessions and a Judaism 101 class. We discussed our plans with a rabbi and priest. We had a beautiful Jewish wedding, with a priest on the platform for good measure. Our ketubah is signed by both Rabbi Sternfield and Father Cimarrusti, and is proudly displayed in our apartment.

And yet, despite Joe's sincere affection for lox and kugel, his ability to spout the occasional Yiddish word (that would make any Jewish grandma proud) and his completely unselfish commitment to raise his children in a religion other than his own—I worry.

The fact is, as much as he accepts and even enjoys Judaism, Joe isn't Jewish.

This became startlingly evident after dinner a few weeks ago, when talk turned to my brother Andy's upcoming move to San Francisco. Andy expressed sadness that he would not get to spend as much time with his future nieces and nephews. This prompted Joe to say, "Well, I guess that takes him off the shortlist for godfather."

Had I replied by saying, "I guess you're right," the conversation would have ended there. But the thought of my Jewish children having a god-father just felt so wrong. Joe's totally offhand comment was shocking to me— and suddenly my head was spinning with questions.

Does Joe want our children to go to church with his parents every Easter? Does he know that I want to start special Shabbat traditions with our children? Will he want to have a Christmas tree in our home? Will he make us sing carols?

After fighting about the godfather issue that night for quite a while, and not coming to any mutually agreeable solution, we let it go for the time being. But the issue hasn't been forgotten, and it makes me wonder what other expectations each of us have that might be a surprise for the other.

My suggestion to honor the prospective godfather by calling him "super fun uncle" was soundly dismissed. Joe's idea of asking someone to serve as godfather and then not really telling anyone about it seems a bit silly. We turned to the internet for ideas, where we stumbled upon a page about the role of the godparent, or Sandek, in Judaism.

As it turns out, Judaism does in fact recognize a godparent, though in a slightly different sense than the traditional Christian godparent. Still, with a little more research, we hope to be able to honor someone in a way that is respectful of both of our religious backgrounds.

But we realize we may not always be that lucky—no matter how much research we do, we're unlikely to find a Jewish Christmas carol or a place for Easter in Judaism. Despite our blanket commitment to raise a Jewish family, we still have different ideas about what exactly a Jewish family is, and how our family will fit into that mold.

The more we talk and ask each other questions, the more apparent it becomes that we may have to make our own mold. We fight at times but we try not to take ourselves too seriously. In the name of compromise, Joe asked me if it would be ok if our (future) dog is Catholic. I can't argue with that.

Despite our dog's religion, Joe has already made up his mind about her name—Kugel Latala.

Alyssa Latala, 30, is the Marketing Communications Manager for a small family foundation. She lives with her husband, Joe, and son, Ben, in suburban Chicago. Her most consistent and meaningful connection to the Jewish community throughout childhood was as a performer. While she no longer performs at the local JCC—or wears suspenders—she is happily singing all kinds of music to Ben, her best audience ever.

This essay was originally published on Oy!Chicago *(www.oychicago.com).*

SUMMER DAYS, SUMMER NIGHTS

By Galit Breen

YOU AND ME, WE'VE TALKED ABOUT THIS BEFORE. You know the rub. There are different ways to do...pretty much everything. Childhood. Mommyhood. Friendships. Relationships. Healthiness. Religiosity. Spirituality. Culture. Love. There are a million-and-one variations. And you know what? They're all right. For someone.

While the ins-and-outs of Judaism vary, Our bread and butter? That's Shabbat.

Nothing screams "Jewish-y," or spirituality for that matter, more to me than the smell of freshly baked challah, the girls' sweet voices saying the blessings over the candles, wine and bread and my son Brody's chubby little fingers holding tightly (oh-so-very-tightly) onto his grape juice.

The family. The fun. The together-ness. The group-sigh-and-deep-exhale in celebration of the weekend being here. Finally. The candlelight, the wine, the flowers, the dialogue, the prayers, the delicious food. Shabbat.

Shabbat comes around every single week (yes, all year long), so it should feel just right. Given that, I've researched, read, attempted, tried again. All to create that "Shabbat-y" feeling for my family. Different. Separate. Special.

One person's Shabbat-iness happens between the walls of a synagogue. And another's between the walls of their own living room. (And perhaps the kitchen.) One person's large gathering, is another's dinner-for-two. One person's prayer well into the night, is another's just-the-basics. One person's fancy-shmancys, is another's comfy-cozies. In my mind, there's not a right way. Just a right feeling.

I have absolutely no shame in admitting that my husband Jason can out-challah braid me. Not a one.

Technically speaking, on Shabbat everything should be prepared in advance so the whole evening can be dedicated to family, spirituality and yummy food. No work. No driving. No other events or activities. No distractions. How beautiful is that?

I love the notion, the sentiment and the pure bliss of it. But in reality, sometimes it's hard to adhere to start times, end times, yays and nays. If it's not what resonates, it starts to feel . . . un-Shabbat-y. There's a technical term for you!

Before Jason and I had children—actually, before we were even married—one of our favorite rabbis asked us how we plan on remembering and observing Shabbat with our (then future, hypothetical) children.

Are you thinking that that was just a little over the top? Not so much, actually. You'd be surprised how many times we've chosen between doing Shabbat at home and an evening out with close friends, a school event or a birthday party. We've always been able to softly land right back on to that conversation.

Why? Because after he posed the question and let it marinate for a little bit, he weighed in. The rabbi's son, a football star, played in Friday night games right after candles were lit and prayers were said. He never had to choose between either of his sparks—Judaism and football. Does this surprise you?

Our rabbi taught us that the Shabbat feeling is peaceful and light. Content and just right. So if you find spirituality by observing every rule and every ritual, that feels beautiful to you. And if you don't? Well then all of that observing and ritual-ing will feel like a burden. Or a restriction. Something to avoid, rather than to envelop within your heart, and take on as your own. I've always remembered that.

Shabbat-y, indeed.

About 10 years and three kids later, I often get my inspiration from play date chit-chats. I've moved from the rabbi's office to a local ice cream shop. I say potato, you say po-tah-to?

This week, my moment-of-clarity happened while my children were becoming increasingly chocolate ice cream smeared, so the conversation was short but powerful. Besides chocolate ice cream (with toppings!), my girlfriend and I discussed how we felt about working versus being at home with our children. Not comparing or weighing options, but reflecting on the idea that when something doesn't feel right, it becomes well, hard. And stressful. And a have-to-do instead of a want-to-do. Not too shabby for two moms over ice cream.

And that brings us right back to Shabbat. And most importantly, creating Shabbat-iness. Many of our Shabbats happen outside. Sometimes we eat a gourmet meal ala Jason. Sometimes we grill. And other times? We have a picnic. Or pizza. That part really doesn't matter. What matters is the connections made, the memories created and the feelings felt.

I am seriously awe-struck by the thought of saying the same words as so many people in so many places. Here, there and everywhere, right? My heart is equally warmed by the thought of baking challah with my children at the same time as other mamas and their babies. Different places, different paths but same warm moments, warm hearts. Sometimes even using the same recipe! That always gives me that warm-and-fuzzy Shabbat-y feeling. Every. Single. Week.

Some families add a set-aside dialogue time during Shabbat. While we haven't broached Torah-topics, we have tried to incorporate a short discussion about something that might have come up for us that week. Kindness. Trying hard. Listening to your mother! Just as a few—ahem—examples.

The Shabbat-iest of Shabbat-iest for me is the moment that I spend whispering something kind, wonderful and appreciative to each of my children. It's not the traditional Hebrew. And it's not the same thing you might say to your children. But it's ours. And it's beautiful. And for us, that feeling can be created just as easily at a fancy table or at a picnic blanket.

Galit Breen is a 35-year-old Israeli freezing her tuchus in Minnesota. On any given day she can be found juggling her husband, three children and new puggle. Galit has a degree in Human Development, a Masters in Education and ten-plus years experience as a classroom teacher. Galit is now a stay-at-home mom, blogger and freelance writer with a serious love for challah. And hummus. And challah with hummus. She is a contributing writer for TC Jewfolk *where she is known as the Minnesota Mamaleh.*

This essay was originally published on TCJewfolk.com.

LIVE, LOVE, LEARN...
BUT IN WHAT ORDER?

By Blair Chavis

THERE IS NOTHING LIKE A JEWISH MOTHER'S LOVE. She loves so deeply that she wants her daughter's life to be filled with love too—but, he must be Jewish.

I was sitting at work late one Tuesday afternoon and my mother called me, her voice filled with adrenaline. She had just come home from the grocery store, and apparently she tried to pick up a little more than milk and eggs.

My mother had just finished getting her groceries into her car and was amused as she watched a "good-looking" Jewish boy doing a juggling act with his. As he picked up three bags, two would drop to the ground.

A Shabbat candle went off in her head, she recalled to me later. The urge to help him was overwhelming.

She called out, "Fella!"

Miraculously, he knew that he was her intended, and had his bags not been weighing him down, he might have run the other way.

My mother shouted out across the parking lot, "Would you like a ride?"

The poor vulnerable soul replied, "Sure."

She got into the car so that she could pull up to him because he couldn't walk to her car. He put his groceries in the back of her station wagon, and he sat down next to her.

As she drove him home she explained that she saw his Michigan t-shirt and it reminded her of her three daughters (who went to Big Ten universities) and "she felt bad for him." She talked about her daughters, while scanning and assessing him to figure out his age, asking him questions about what he did, etc. She didn't want to allocate him to the wrong daughter.

She learned that he was in graduate school for journalism at Northwestern University's Medill program and she zeroed in on me. He talked about his studies and she told him I'm a reporter.

She scrambled, telling him about my work, as they approached his apartment and said, "I should have you meet my daughter!"

He laughed and said, "Right"—as if they were both joking. He got out of the car and got his bags and peeked his head back in the window and said, "Have her come and visit me at Medill." He shook her hand, thanked her and went on his way.

Thankfully, my mother couldn't follow through, as she often has successfully attempted to match my sisters in the past. When I say successfully, I mean she has succeeded in actually giving out our phone numbers to strange, "good looking" Jewish boys.

With a mensch whispering in her ear from one shoulder and a yenta shouting at her from the other, the mensch won. She admitted that she didn't want to look like she was doing him a favor just for him to meet her daughter—though that had been her intention.

"I turned out to be a decent person in the end," she laughed. "I preferred he think there is some decency in this world and that I didn't have ulterior motives."

My mother has the warmest heart of anyone I know, and truly wants the best for her daughters. When she finished her story, she was genuinely disappointed in herself that she didn't succeed with this one.

"It was a short ride," she added.

I, however, was horrified and laughing at the same time.

My sisters and I have faced many matchmaker attempts from both of our parents. I know that I am part of a sisterhood of women whose parents also subtly or not so subtly try to set them up.

In general, secular societal attitudes about women have markedly changed since our parents' era, but some Jewish mothers are still sending a strong message: Why aren't you married yet?

Whether they're kidding or half-kidding or not kidding at all, it puts some of us in an awkward fix.

Some young Jewish women I know are happily entering into matrimony, others aren't ready yet. Those who are pursuing multiple degrees or trying to navigate their careers throughout their 20s may not yet have marriage on the brain. Young professionals move for jobs. Ask any journalist, for instance, how many times they have to move cities and markets to move up the media ladder?

That being said, it's sometimes hard for a young woman to build a nest with someone else when she's still trying to find her own roots.

Blair Chavis has been a contributing blogger for www.oychicago. com since 2009 and has loved every moment of it. It is only fitting that she is an Oy!Chicago contributor, as "oy" is one of the most frequently uttered words in her vocabulary, according to her co-workers, friends and family. She is 27 years old and grew up in Highland Park, IL, now residing in Chicago where she works as an editor for Prime Publishing LLC, editing and managing food websites.

This essay was originally published on Oy!Chicago (www.oychicago.com).

MY (JEWISH-INTERFAITH-LESBIAN) WEDDING

By Chai Wolfman

CHANGE IS POSSIBLE. WHEN I FIRST CAME OUT TO MY grandmother, she told me that she was okay with it, but didn't agree with gay marriage. Several years later, this same grandmother actually hosted our wedding at her home.

At our wedding, there were those who refused to call it a wedding. Relatives with George W. Bush bumper stickers parked next to friends counting down to the end of his reign. There were Christians, Jews, Buddhists and those embracing their own self-defined spirituality or none at all. Some guests came who only speak the words "lesbian" or "gay" in whispers—and only when they find themselves unable to avoid it altogether—while other friends and family who embrace our relationship wrote heartfelt blessings for us as part of our ceremony.

Mandi and I started dating in college when we were both 20 and quickly became inseparable. After being completely in love for five years, she proposed. We spent two years planning our wedding—partly to take our time and enjoy the process, partly because July 2007 had a good ring to it and partly to give our families time to get used to the idea.

People didn't know how to respond to our decision to have a wedding. We had to listen to some say they didn't agree with us. We only received one engagement present.

We had to create a ceremony from scratch. We had to figure out how to respond to people who didn't understand what we meant when we told them we were getting married. We dealt with the traditional drama of who to invite and not to invite. We spent loads of cash. Why were we doing this again?

For all of these reasons and more. Because creating our own ceremony gave me the opportunity to question which Jewish traditions were important to me and had meaning for both of us as an interfaith couple. Because through the entire process of planning and figuring out how to deal with some hard questions we grew more resilient as individuals and stronger as a couple. Because by being open about our love, we let people into our lives and allowed our families to embrace us in a way that didn't seem possible before.

And because it was FUN! Because roasting s'mores over a bonfire and dancing with your closest friends and relatives in the middle of a meadow on a clear summer night creates the best memories. Because maybe we could help people leave their judgments in the past and open their minds to others who are different from themselves. Because despite everyone's differences, there was not a dry eye at the end of our ceremony and I will never forget my grandmother hugging me afterward and saying, "You are such a good lesson for all of us."

I know not everyone is open to learning these lessons. Mandi's mom did not come to our wedding. She did not acknowledge the invitation we sent. She did not ask us about the preparations or to see the pictures afterward. She still does not see our relationship for what it is. There is no getting around how much that hurts, but there is nothing I can do to change it.

The best I can do is to continue caring about her and focusing on the good things she does bring into my life. We are all human beings, after all. In acknowledging this and being true to ourselves as individuals and as a couple, Mandi and I hope to help others to do the same.

In this small way, we are working together toward the promise we made at the end of our ketubah: that together we will help build a world filled with peace and love. I cannot think of a better way to do this as an interfaith lesbian couple than to live every day openly, embracing differences and common humanity with kindness and compassion. I know this will not be an easy task, but my experience so far has shown me that facing the challenge is worth it.

One week after the big day, the very same grandmother who once voiced her opposition to gay marriage was excitedly suggesting sperm donors so we can start our family. Really, Grandma, one thing at a time.

Chai Wolfman, 30, is an artist, writer, cellist, and former Jewish nonprofit professional, a role she recently left in order to spend more time with her children. Growing up in the tiny Jewish community of Appleton, Wisconsin has left her only mildly useful in playing Jewish geography. Chai lives in Chicago with her partner, Mandi, and their twin daughters, Violet and Autumn.

This essay was originally published on Oy!Chicago (www.oychicago.com).

HEBREW NAMES.
OR, DREAMING OF VARDIT

By Vicki Boykis

I RECENTLY READ AN ARTICLE IN *TABLET*, A GREAT NEW Jewish web magazine, on "cool" new Hebrew names to give your kids. Because now, apparently, Jacob and Hannah are overrated. This made me think back to the time I got my Hebrew name. It's a sordid tale, so you might want to snack on some hummus, Jacob and Hannah, as you read.

A lot of people I know were born with Hebrew names. On every organized trip to Israel I've been on, roll call has often been full of Hannahs, Esthers, and Michaels. And maybe an Avi or two. But because I was born in the extremely anti-Semitic Soviet Union and my parents didn't want me to catch an ass-kicking every now and again, not to mention that my dad isn't Jewish, they decided on a non-Hebrew name for me, Victoria. You can see that drama unfold here.

When I was 17 and went on a March of the Living trip to Poland and Israel, for the first time in my life, I really started feeling Jewish. I asked a bunch of questions of the kids on my trip who had grown up in Jewish homes, an experience I had never had. There was one person on my trip that I pestered the most, a woman in her 50s or 60s, with grandchildren a little younger than me, Susan. Susan was a typical New York Jew, and, for me, a real blessing because she understood the Russian kids on the trip all too well.

She knew we were brought up to sneer on any kind of events with religious overtones, to eat pork, and were in ignorance of 90% of Jewish traditions.

It wasn't our fault, or our parents' fault. It's just what Russian Jews did to survive the Soviet Union. With patience, she explained to me what Shabbat was and why we celebrated it when I expressed my complete unwillingness at having to visit a synagogue for services in Poland. She showed me how to wash my hands before a meal when I shied away in terror from a ritual all the other kids were performing with knowledge. And she answered my constant questions about the subject I was most interested in, Hebrew.

"So, you say ha before every word in Hebrew?" I asked her. "No, it's like the word 'the'."

"So, how do you say, 'I love Israel?'" "Well, it depends on if it's a masculine or feminine 'I.' I would say, 'Ani, Shoshana, ohevet et Israel.'" I asked her why she pointed to herself as Shoshana. "It's my Hebrew name," she said.

My curiosity in Hebrew names was piqued. It also helped that there were at least 10 Russian kids on our bus, Hebrew name-less. In addition to me, there were also the likes of Svetlana, Irina, Igor, and Kirill (probably the most ironically named of all, because Kirill is Russian for St. Cyril). Susan and our Russian shaliach decided it would be a great opportunity to give us all Hebrew names on our first time in Israel, seeing how attached we were getting to being Jewish. That was the good part.

The bad part was that none of us really knew Hebrew at a level well enough to understand the name we were receiving. I thumbed through the Hebrew name book (in Hebrew, of course,) with the shaliach. "You know that receiving a new name changes the direction of your life," he said casually. He would know. He'd made aliyah when he was 16 and changed his Russian name to a Hebrew one a year later. I looked at the foreign letters with trepidation. What if I messed up and chose the wrong one? Would that mean I would be banished to the West Bank, or worse, Dimona?

"What's the name that's closest to Victoria or Victory in Hebrew," I asked him.

"Probably Nitzana. But you don't want that name. It doesn't sound nice." And of course, it didn't to me. I listened to whatever he told me.

He kept thumbing, no doubt past many desirable choices like Raheli or Goldameirit. "Vered," he said. "It's close-sounding to your name. What do you think about that?"

I thought it sounded pretty awesome. I didn't realize that it had the same connotations in Hebrew as Ethel. No offense to anyone named Vered. It's not like you could have chosen your own name. Unlike some people that are writing this post.

"It sounds pretty cool! What does it mean?"

"Rose."

I thought this over in my mind. I had none of the characteristics I thought girls with flower names were supposed to have. I didn't get regular mani/pedi combos. I didn't know the difference between rouge and foundation. And I wasn't gentle, understanding, and lady-like, a trait I imagined all girls with flower names shared. I was definitely not a Vered.

"I'll take it," I said, and was proclaimed Vered the next day on a hill overlooking the Kinneret. It was all very nationalistic. I might have cried. Or maybe those were just Jewllergies. But about a year after I got the name, I started Hebrew classes at my university. And then I got jealous. Some people were Shulamit, or Anat, or Keren. I cursed myself. Why couldn't I have even chosen Vardit? That would sound at least a little bit cooler. But no, from that day forward, I was Vered. It got so bad that, when I did an internship at Bank HaPoalim in Israel and I was being introduced to my coworkers, I said, "Shmi Vered," and they said, "Shmech WHAT?" And I said, "Shmaybe not." After that, I was Vicki the whole summer.

Me, Vered-less, in my Poalim office. You can tell it's Israel in the summer because I look like I just came out of a tanning booth. Five times.

I can't even use my Hebrew name in the Land of Israel. The ultimate Zionist failure. If there are any Vereds out there that are proud of our name, please come forward. Otherwise I will keep dreaming of being Orly or Yael forever.

Born in wayback Soviet Russia, Vicki grew up in Pennsylvania and graduated with Honors in Economics, a minor in Hebrew, and a certificate in Nerdry from Penn State University. She's married to a man who was brave enough to propose to her at the Spanish Synagogue in Prague, earning him major Jew points from her mom. After living and working in the DC metro area for the past three years, she is currently working as a consultant in Philadelphia. She blogs about all of this at blog.vickiboykis.com

This essay was originally published on Jewlicious.

CAN YOU DATE ME NOW? GOOD

By Matt Lash

AUNT ELLEN IS A P-I-M-P. PIMP. ON NANA LASH'S 70-something birthday ("Nana" is what my family calls our grandmothers, and to be honest, she could be 100 years old but I can't tell old-peoples' ages), I sent her a card, my parents sent her some money and flowers, my brother sent her beer bread (because he for some reason thinks she likes beer bread, weird), but nothing could beat what Howard gave her. Howard gave her a cordless phone. It was her first cordless phone ever, and not only did he give her the phone, he taught her how to use it! What a man Howard is, especially since he can drive at night, which is apparently a big thing for the old Jewish women in the suburbs. How else will they get to their Mahjhong games?

Who's Howard? Howard is Aunt Ellen's gift to Nana Lash, through JDate. For the Jewish folk, JDate has become our mother's new best friend, and the answer to her question, "So when are you going to meet a nice Jewish girl?" Aunt Ellen didn't find Nana Lash a nice, Jewish girl, but instead she found her Howard. The world has actually turned ass-up when my Nana has been pimped online to find a Jewish man who can drive at night. But that's where we stand in our dating practices; the world has gotten too big and sexual harassment charges are so rampant, you can't flirt anymore! (That's a joke, by the way...sexual harassment is bad).

So we go to online dating. And EVERYONE is doing online dating. Searching online, I found dating sights for farmers (www.farmersonly.com), Jews (jdate.com, jlove.com, and I'm sure there's more), and the most ironic one, a dating site for conservatives (conservativematch.com). Doesn't it seem funny to you that a group with such focused and "high moral values" search a database of women (or men) who are publicly airing out their information? I always thought conservative meant NOT being public about your social life; isn't "repression now, ascension later," like, their slogan?

Oh, and don't worry, gold-diggers, there's a site for you too. www.seekingarrangment.com fuses the obnoxious with the superficial by networking rich men or women with "sugar babies." If you're a hot guy or girl that wants to get pampered by Daddy Warbucks, this is your site; just leave your dignity at the door (that goes for you as well, Warbucks!).

And while I've never used JDate, I will admit to online dating before. I've done it twice, and it turned out hilariously entertaining. Not because I found my soulmate, but mostly because of the trainwreck of a situation it turned out to be. I'm not going to get into the details of my dates, but I will tell you that when a girl messages you on www.myspace.com, "Hey, you're hot," it's not going to be one of those lasting relationships that you're going to want to tell Nana Lash and Howard about.

So I've listed off five or more sites for people to go and do their thang in the dating scene, but while searching the sites, I never came across a sight that really hits home. Guys, we spend loads of money getting girls to like us, basically because we know that we're worthless, but hope to bribe women into looking the other way and "settling" for our presence. Dating sites that focus on religion, sexual preference, sexual deviance (for the conservatives, of course) and the like all miss the big point: cell-phone charges.

I've spent hundreds of dollars dating outside of my plan. When my mother asks me, "When are you going to date a nice, Jewish girl?" my response is, "As soon as I find one with a Verizon plan." All of those day-time phone calls, telling the person you miss them or that they smell pretty, those minutes add up! And people can overcome religious differences, I mean it's not THAT hard, right Jews and [insert any other religion or philosophical belief]? But we hold cell-phone service plans as close to our hearts as we do our secret book of poetry that we hide in our closet next to the bathroom, fourth shelf behind the autobiography of Motley Crue. Or at least I hold cell-phone service that dearly.

That being said, I'm proposing a new dating website, dedicated to what means the most, and that's my cell-phone minutes from 8 a.m. until 9 p.m. If you're not in my plan, you're not in my PLAN. Maybe something like "Cellmatch.com" or "wirelesslovers.com." I mean, we all don't have Aunt Ellen to pimp us out like she did for Nana Lash, so if I'm going to do it myself, then I want to be sure it's not costing me my daytime minutes!

Matt Lash, a 2007 graduate of Chicago-Kent College of Law, died April 30, 2008 at age 27 after a seven and a half year battle with Ewing's sarcoma, a rare form of bone cancer. Matt left a lasting mark on the people he met, both through law school and his Birthright Israel trip.

This essay was originally published in Chicago Kent Law School's The Commentator *in October of 2006.*

THE INTELLECTUAL GIVER

By Emily Keeler

FREELANCING. THE WORD FREE IS ACTUALLY IN THE JOB title. Free from the 9-to-5 days, free to daydream, free to drink two pots of coffee a day in pajamas while earning a glossy name for yourself in high-visibility magazines. But freelance writing requires perseverance and is not necessarily fun or reliable work.

Overeducated and unemployed in Jerusalem, I tapped into online freelance writing opportunities. I soon discovered, however, that cyberspace primarily coughs up mundane topics for writers who dredge up sentences for measly pay. That is, until I connected with thousands of anonymous voices desperate for my words.

On the brink of financial desperation, I caught a break. I received a simple email that read: "Are you still interested in writing for us?" The woman from the company called to explain that I would receive up to 50 emails a day with "model research paper" topics. I would have the liberty to write whichever ones I wanted, according to my resources, time, and mood.

I soon realized that writing "model research papers" meant writing term papers for students as bankrupt intellectually as I was financially. I mitigated my ethical concern by calculating it as an exchange: You need a paper, and I write it. It's supply and demand. Besides, once I release a paper, I have no control over its destiny. If my clients are submitting my work as their own, the burden weighs on their own shoulders. Still, something about the whole business seems bizarre. When I talk about my job, the range of reactions I receive includes astonishment, disapproval, envy, and even offers of payment for me to finish graduate-level papers. When people ask what I do, I boast "freelance," and then avert my eyes and gaze into a swirling drink.

Yet with no other job prospects, I began to willingly bear the pressure of deadlines for strangers. Each day I sit down to write clear and concise essays on American literature and biblical studies, my fingers skimming the black and white keys like a pianist's, deep in meditative rhythm. Then the truth hit me. I realized that I love my job. I love writing research papers without going to class or worrying about the grade. I love digging up my old literature anthologies and coming up with new ideas without taking responsibility for them. My anonymous clients and I form a clandestine relationship, the complicit silence of cyberspace our witness.

Six months after receiving that fateful email, I found a weekly Jewish e-newsletter sandwiched between paper requests. It contained an article titled "What Harm?" by Eliyahu Safran, and it was about gneivat daat, or intellectual theft. I wondered if signs exist, and what to do when I get signs I don't want to read. It began: "What harm in the student altering an answer on an exam in order to avoid a failing grade? Or copying a couple of paragraphs from an article in order to complete an assignment?" Then it continued: "A gonev daat is one who intentionally misleads or gives a false impression through his words or deeds. It does not matter if 'no one is harmed' or if the dishonesty was not actually witnessed by one's fellow. It is always and absolutely wrong."

By definition, my clients are the gnevei daat, intellectual bandits making off in the night with my thoughts and perfect citations. I may have never plagiarized, but am I complicit in a crime against God?

The complication with academic writing is that it doesn't always seem wrong. There are times I believe I am helping a struggling student. Among my virtual clientele I imagine a middle-aged nurse juggling a family and a career. A foreign student swamped with English assignments. In fact, some of the people I turned to for ethical advice expressed approval for students who occasionally pass off busywork that does not advance their skills. Part of the responsibility for this thriving phenomenon, some say, lay with professors who do not take the time to get to know their students' work. On a theoretical plane, there is a camp that says academic writing can be understandable, if not excusable.

Yet Safran's rabbinical perspective delineates black from white for our grayscale American society. The problem of intellectual theft is less about theft, and more about deception. The trivial lies we all tell—from inquiring about goods we have no intention of buying to bestowing a disingenuous compliment—"are worse than blatant lies, precisely because of their hidden nature." In the grayscale picture, my clients are not bona fide thieves: I sold them the rights to my work. What is wrong, from the vantage point of gneivat daat, is that they use my words to deceive their readers.

We may agree that lying and plagiarizing are wrong. However, a theory of moral relativity allows us to let those half-lies and questionable deceptions slip by, even when our intuitions hint otherwise. Our intellects rationalize the gentle tug on the dial of our moral compasses from true north. We're not wrong. It's just the tides. It seems that our society has allowed the smudging of moral boundaries as part of the human experience and the American spirit of letting nothing hold us back from success. According to Safran, "Such a laissez faire attitude might carry the day amongst those for whom honesty and dishonesty are not character traits but tolerable—and equally allowable—strategies for getting ahead in the world; to be employed as the situation dictates and used for advantage." Without sturdy fences around right and wrong, moral relativity prevails.

The American politicians and athletes of late, whose nearsighted vision sought personal gratification, are reminders of the downside of this cultural phenomenon. As Jews, we are called to agree with Safran when he says, "there is a reason that laissez faire is a language other than Hebrew." But moreover, maybe the men in this meteor shower of fallen stars never imagined their original sins would amount to the gravity of their falls. As they deceived their partners and themselves, their insidious lies snowballed into an avalanche. Deception is integral to extramarital affairs, and that, perhaps, is why we call it cheating.

If nothing else, Safran is correct that "A misdeed is always witnessed. Perhaps not by a fellow, but certainly by God. And most certainly by one's own heart." In the sea of subjectivity, the essence of gneivat daat— deceiving somebody—is ultimately deceiving oneself.

Although the paper-writing business will go on without me, I hope someday soon to leave it behind, to raise the bar with all the other dreamers of a good and honest world. When that day comes, I will miss the best job I've ever had.

Emily Keeler, 30, has moved away from the term paper industry and is now a successful freelance writer and editor for reputable publications. Originally from Mystic, CT, she holds a B.A. from Northeastern University, a Master of Theological Studies from Harvard Divinity School, and has studied at the Hebrew University of Jerusalem and the Conservative Yeshiva. Among her many aspirations, she plans to write a vegan Passover cookbook and holiday how-to manual for young adults. She lives in Seattle with her husband.

This essay was originally published in PresentTense *Magazine*

SORRY I DON'T TOUCH MEN: TRUE CONFESSIONS OF A CELIBATE DATER

By Marcy Rivka Nehorai

ANY MOMENT NOW, IT'S GOING TO RING.

I'm watching my phone.

My body is preparing itself to receive two words emphatically digitally shrieked from the confines of a New Jersey suburban home: "I'm engaged!!!"

One of my closest friends has flown to the other side of our beloved country to meet the family of the man she has concluded is her beshert. A long distance relationship, they have only actually met four times, for multiple days each visit, in the last six weeks.

Welcome to the world of frum dating. I'll be your guide.

For starters, a common term associated with frum dating is shomer negiyah (guarding touch), meaning that the couple desists from any physical activity—including handshakes, hugs, etc—until after the chuppah. Which also means delayed gratification for the impatient among us.

Myself a Baal Teshuva (someone who became observant later in life), I became shomer negiyah five years ago, when I was 20, with curiosity about the way it would change my relationships with men. Growing up, I was ignorant of any Jewish rules regarding sexuality. Not aware there was even an option of anything different—

who would agree to a nonphysical romantic relationship?—I cheerfully chose a lifestyle similar to my peers.

Though I had more or less healthy relationships, I am deeply cognizant of the scars these decisions left behind. Now I observe the positive impact physical boundaries can have on the emotional and psychological growth of a couple. I am a walking witness to the workings of both worlds.

I am reminded about a night a few months ago when I attended my friend's birthday party at a Chicago bar. Explaining that I don't touch men to one who approached me, I had to reassure him that I was not a victim to the delusions of an oppressive religious doctrine. Motioning to the ladies chatting around us, thin layers of fabric occasionally covering parts of their body, I grinned and assured him that though externally I am more restrained than in my past, internally I am living joyfully the greatest time of my life.

My eyes return to the silent phone, and I text her a simple, concerned "How are you?" I wonder why the news hasn't yet hit.

To meet a potential spouse, I might go to a coworker, rabbi, teacher, friend, or anyone who knows anyone in the religious community, and tell them what I am looking for. I have a resume I sometimes send out to shidduch (dating) groups who try to pair up people. The resume includes my personal history, where I stand religiously, what I offer and what I am looking for. The person who does the matchmaking is called the shadchan. Many times, I've researched into a potential spouse with given references to inquire about the person's past and compatibility.

With this style of dating, those who enter this focused arena are aware they won't receive the perks of the noncommittal, let's-wake-up-in-bed-next-to-each-other-for-two-years-and-then-maybe-we-will-be-ready-for-the-marriage-talk relationship. Thus, the intensity level for men and women on discerning their needs and commitment usually matches. With any confusion, the shadchan can be called, to offer advice or to call the other party to address any concerns. The infamous male/female divide is bridged slightly by the in-between who volunteers his or her services to bring clarity to the situation as quickly and comfortably as possible.

There is no standardization; the number of dates varies by each couple. My previous roommate went on seven dates over the span of two weeks before deciding to engage. Others will go on 10 dates, 20 dates; no proper measurement exists. Without physical interaction, which often delays cutting off an ill-suited pair, and having a well-matched team decide on their future, the process is often quicker.

I will not suggest that frum dating is painless. In fact, it most often is a deeply painful process of feeling judged, being rejected, rejecting others, waiting, trying to smile when others succeed, falling into despair, reminding yourself of who you are, brushing off the debris, standing back up, and re-dialing your shadchan's phone number to reestablish your availability in the market.

However, the perks of such a system are, without a doubt in my mind, immense. It is impossible to understand the glory of such a system without experiencing it, just as it is impossible to fully know the emptiness of a world until you leave it behind for a more satisfying existence. These days I think about my previous lifestyle and revel in my increased level of calm, joy, and clarity. In a society obsessed with youth, all I can say is thank goodness I have aged.

I glance at the phone still lying silently beside me.

In the system my friend and I have chosen, all we can do is keep our hopes high, be as levelheaded as possible, and hurry up and wait for the Almighty to do what He does best. We are determined not to be left behind as we clamor to participate in this volatile ride. We are convinced that the seats we have chosen to get us to where we need to be are, in the end, the smartest, smoothest, and most enjoyable ones available.

Marcy Rivka Nehorai, 26, grew up in the flat plains of Midwest suburbia, in Jewish Country—Highland Park, Illinois. Currently she lives in Israel with her husband as he gets his Master's degree in Jewish Education. She spends her time studying at the Mayanot Institute for Jewish Studies, and participating in the Jerusalem art scene. Her works can be viewed at naftaliart.com. She is invested in the power of art as a tool for expression, raising awareness, and social commentary. It is her career goal to work in actualizing this potential, in herself and others. She is also a huge fan of gefilte fish.

This essay was originally published on Oy!Chicago (www.oychicago.com).

EPILOGUE

I SET OUT ON THIS JOURNEY TO TRY TO ANSWER some of the questions the Jewish communal world has raised about Jewish 20- and 30-somethings—how we live Jewishly, how to engage us, what makes us tick. And I've learned that the answers are not so black and white.

I've also learned that when you embark on a journey like this one, there are inevitably going to be surprises along the way. The first surprise came early on with the initial influx of emails I received after sending out my call for submissions. I honestly couldn't believe how many people were expressing an interest in what I was doing. But what was most surprising—and to me, most telling—was how many people thanked *me* for this opportunity; thanked *me* for giving them a voice. Before I had even read the first submission, I knew I was onto something.

I was also surprised to see stories that reflected some discrepancies from the research I have done about this generation: Instead of stories of disinterest in Jewish ritual and tradition, I read stories of meaningful Jewish engagement and personal connection to ritual; instead of stories of disinterest in Israel, I read stories of connection to the Hebrew language (I was surprised, however not to have received any stories about Birthright Israel, considering the impact and success of the initiative among this age group); instead of stories about intermarriage, I read several stories of conversion. I also read many stories about relationships, community, and defining identity, and I believe many of the essays reflect a cultural shift that is not unique to the Jewish community but rather a general shift in American ideology.

It is noteworthy to mention that a vast majority of the submissions came from young adults who work in the Jewish communal world or write for Jewish blogs or publications. In retrospect, this is not so surprising. Perhaps, though not its intention, this collection will provide a window into the rising generation of Jewish communal leaders and professionals, especially coinciding with the release of two recent studies on this subject matter: "*Jewish Communal Professionals in North America: A Profile,*" a study by Steven M. Cohen released in November of 2010 and "Generations of Change: How Leaders in their Twenties and Thirties are Reshaping American Jewish Life," a study released in September 2010 by Jack Wertheimer, referenced in the Prologue. This anthology hopefully gives some personal narrative to those published conclusions.

So where do we go from here? Through this journey, I think I've answered some questions and uncovered other questions about this generation of Jews that will be answered in time. Perhaps future research will collect personal essays written by non-communal professionals or look deeper into issues such as what Zionism means to this generation, the effects of post-denominationalism, or the changing face of Judaism amid greater cultural shifts in the general population. And although I don't think I've solved the mystery of our elusive generation, I do have some insights into the types of stories we want to tell.

However it is that we young Jews express ourselves Jewishly, I'm certain that every Jewish 20- or 30-something has an interesting story—and maybe all we need is the opportunity to tell it.

SUBJECT INDEX FOR ESSAYS

Acknowledgments

I would like to thank my colleagues and friends at the Jewish United Fund/Jewish Federation of Metropolitan Chicago for their support and encouragement, particularly Cheryl Jacobs and Linda Haase, and a very special thanks to Aaron Cohen, for making this book possible.

I would also like to thank the Spertus Institute of Jewish Studies, particularly Barry Chazan and my cohort in the Master of Arts in Jewish Professional Studies program. It was an honor and an inspiration to study among and learn from all of you. Special thanks to Rabbi Scott Aaron and Rabbi Josh Feigelson for their guidance in this process.

And finally, thanks to my family—Mom, Dad and Lonnie— and my husband Mike, for your constant and unconditional love and support.

Of special note are the following publications from which many of the essays included in this collection originated:

Huffington Post, *eJewishPhilanthropy*, *Detroit Jewish News*, *Jewcy.com*. *Oy!Chicago* (www.oychicago.com), *The Washington Jewish Week*, *Bustedhalo.com*, *CJ: Voices of Conservative/Masorti Judaism*, New York Jewish Week's *Text/Context*, the anthology *What We Brought Back*, the anthology *The Best Women's Travel Writing of 2011*, *www.nextgenJews.org*, *Jewlicious*, *RJ.org*, *Zeek*, *TC Jewfolk*, Chicago Kent Law School's *The Commentator*, and *PresenTense* Magazine.

www.ingramcontent.com/pod-product-compliance
Lightning Source LLC
Chambersburg PA
CBHW052131270326
41930CB00012B/2847